saint
of the
Day

A Life and Lesson
for Each
of the 173 saints
of the New Missal

Edited by Leonard Foley, O.F.M.

Nihil Obstat:
    Rev. Hilarion Kistner, O.F.M.
    Rev. John J. Jennings

Imprimi Potest:
    Rev. Roger Huser, O.F.M.
    Provincial

Imprimatur:
    + Joseph L. Bernardin
    Archbishop of Cincinnati
    August 13, 1974

The *Nihil Obstat* and *Imprimatur* are a declaration that a book or pamphlet is considered to be free from doctrinal or moral error. It is not implied that those who have granted the *Nihil Obstat* and *Imprimatur* agree with the contents, opinions, or statements expressed.

Woodcuts by John Quigley, O.F.M.
Cover design by Michael Reynolds

SBN-0-912228-16-4

© 1974 St. Anthony Messenger Press
All rights reserved.
Printed in the U.S.A.

CONTENTS

EX LIBRIS
RICARDO C. CASTELLANOS

INTRODUCTION

A loving God offers us his friendship, and the result of that gracious act is our holiness.

God alone is holy: to be God is to be holy. Not to be God is not to be holy. It is not "right" or "natural" for man to live the life of God. But God creates his own life in us, and makes it "right" for him to love us. Why? Because he finds his own life and love in us: it becomes "natural" for us to live "supernatural" or divine lives.

This was God's eternal plan: "God chose us in Christ before the world began to be holy and blameless in his sight, to be full of love." "I am the Vine, you are the branches. He who lives in me and I in him, will produce abundantly, for without me you can do nothing."

With faith, all this is obvious. Without faith, it contradicts obvious human experience. A prime heresy of all ages has been the one that says holiness is what man creates by his own efforts.

It seems so evident that it was *my* strength of character that refused to take revenge; *my* hard-won decision to remain faithful in marriage; *my* endurance that brought me to Mass every Sunday; *my* devotion that prompts me to fast twice a week and give tithes of all I possess. Why shouldn't I thank God that I'm not like the rest of men—at least many of them?

Faith is the answer.

Faith is not a naive abandonment of reason to certain mysterious "truths," nor a feverish scrambling to put together a respectable life of "good works." Faith is the gift whereby we are able to receive a gift. We are able to open ourselves to God's friendship, communion, oneness. Our freedom becomes total freedom when we let Christ enfold it in his own.

It is true that we must "work" at being holy, keeping the commandments, being on the alert for others' need, disciplining ourselves. But even this effort is God's gift, and the more we realize it the more we will use the gift. We have absolutely nothing to give God — except himself.

The supreme example of human holiness is that which Jesus received — *as true man* — from his Father. His heart was totally open to the gift of his Father's love, and by his death and resurrection he is the living source whereby the *Holy* Spirit flows into us and through us.

The saints whose lives are described in this book are *special* signs of God's activity. Their surrender to God's love was so generous an approach to the total surrender of Jesus that the Church recognized them as heroes and heroines worthy to be held up for our inspiration. They remind us that the Church *is* holy, can never stop being holy, is called to show the holiness of God by living the life of Christ.

Our holiness is the same as theirs — God's holiness. Their lives were indeed conditioned by the culture and history of their own day; their expression of holiness is partly different from what it would be in the 20th century. But the essence is the same: they received God's gift with joy. They call to us to do the same.

Are you not aware that you are the temple of God and that the Spirit of God dwells in you? If anyone destroys God's temple, God will destroy him. For the temple of God is holy, and you are that temple. (I Cor. 3:16-17).

LEGENDS AND FACTS

It is evident that there are two kinds of biography of saints. First, there is "practical hagiography" ("hagios" — "holy" and "graphein" — "to write"). From earliest times lists of martyrs were drawn up so that their anniversaries could be remembered. There were also narratives of martyrdom written by contemporaries of the martyrs. Finally, there were accounts written by later writers to edify or to satisfy curiosity. Collections were made, finally developing into what were called legendaries.

Scientific hagiography began in the 17th century. A Jesuit, Rosweyde, first conceived the project of a collection of the lives of the saints. The project was actually carried out by J. Bollandus (hence the name

Bollandists). As much as the state of historical science then permitted, the material of the lives of the saints was subjected to severe critical analysis. Later, with the development in archeology, philology and paleography, greater advances were made in determining the factual content of saints' biographies.

In this book we have clearly labeled *legend* as such. We have included the legendary material because it is part of the tradition (small "t") of the Church. Ages previous to ours were not blessed (or afflicted) with our passion for scientific historical accuracy. Whether this saint actually walked on the water or not, whether the sacred host flew from the hands of the priest to the saint's heart or not, was of no real concern. God had worked infinitely greater miracles of grace in the lives of these heroes and heroines of Christ. If what we call legendary is not factually true, it is often true to the character and spirit of the saint involved. In short, if it didn't happen, it easily could have.

We have kept and identified some of the legends, therefore, as the quaint and human poetry of countless ordinary Christians whose imaginations knew no bounds when God's friendship with his holy ones was involved.

IF YOU LIKE STATISTICS

There are 173 saints commemorated by name in the new Roman Missal. Of these, 145 are men, 28 are women. In the present mood of society, it seems neither necessary or useful to comment on that fact!

The list indicates that the Church has experienced its greatest inspiration from its martyrs and its spiritual and intellectual leaders, as may be seen from the following list:

49 martyrs	5 abbots
43 bishops	4 evangelists
30 doctors	3 deacons
31 priests	2 parents
15 popes	1 hermit
14 virgins	1 worker
14 apostles	1 husband
8 religious	1 monk

Obviously there are more religious, workers, husbands and wives than are named as such. The relative scarcity of laymen, however, is as striking as that of women.

Eleven saints are untitled. Six are royalty. The other five are Martha, Mary Magdalen, Monica, Jerome Emiliani and Francis of Assisi.

KINDS OF CELEBRATION

The highest class of liturgical celebration is the *Solemnity* (formerly the First Class feast). There are three, among celebrations of saints' days: Joseph, Peter and Paul, John the Baptist.

The next class consists of *Feasts* (formerly Second Class feasts). Saints' days celebrated as feasts are those of the apostles, Paul, Mark, Luke, Stephen, Lawrence.

Memorials are former Third Class feasts. About one third of the saints' days are *obligatory* memorials, i.e., they must be celebrated unless superseded by a higher ranking celebration (e.g., a day of Lent). The other celebrations of saints' days are *optional*.

AUTHORS

This book is the result of a cooperative effort of the following Franciscan friars of St. John the Baptist Province and the staff of St. Anthony Messenger.

Alan Hirt
Aldric Heidlage
Anthony Panozzo
Anthony Walter
Austin Ernstes
Bede Clancy
Berard Doerger
Boniface Sack
Christopher Kerr
Cletus Kistner
Gary Sabourin
George Darling
George Miller
Hilarion Kistner
Jeffrey Scheeler
Jerome Kaelin
Jerome Kircher
John Bach
John Boehman

Joseph Ricchini
Lawrence Landini
Leander Blumlein
Michael Wohler
Murray Bodo
Nicholas Lohkamp
Norbert Oldegeering
Patrick McCloskey
Peter Poppleton
Peter Ricke
Pio O'Connor
Robert Buescher
Roy Effler
Steve Connair
Timothy Carmody
William Faber
William Farris
William Linesch

Contributing members of St. Anthony Messenger staff:

Jeremy Harrington
Leonard Foley
Jack Wintz

Norman Perry
Lisa Biedenbach
Mary Lynne Rapien

TABLE OF ILLUSTRATIONS

All illustrations by John Quigley, O.F.M.

BASIL THE GREAT and GREGORY NAZIANZEN, bishops and doctors

Basil the Great (329-379)

Basil was on his way to becoming a famous teacher when he decided to begin a religious life of Gospel poverty. After studying various modes of religious life, he founded what was probably the first monastery in Asia Minor. He is to monks of the East what St. Benedict is to the West, and his principles influence Eastern monasticism today.

He was ordained priest, assisted the Archbishop of Caesarea, (now southeastern Turkey) and ultimately became archbishop himself, in spite of opposition from some of his suffragan bishops, probably because they foresaw coming reforms.

One of the most damaging heresies in the history of the Church, Arianism, which denied the divinity of Christ, was at its height. The emperor Valens persecuted the orthodox, and put great pressure on Basil to remain silent and admit the heretics to communion. Basil remained firm, and Valens backed down. But trouble remained. When the great St. Anthanasius died, the mantle of defender of the faith against Arianism fell upon Basil. He strove mightily to unite and rally his fellow Catholics who were crushed by tyranny and torn by internal dissension. He was misunderstood, misrepresented, accused of heresy and ambition. Even appeals to the Pope brought no response. "For my sins I seem to be unsuccessful in everything."

He was tireless in pastoral care. He preached twice a day to huge crowds, built a hospital that was called a wonder of the world (as a youth he had organized famine relief and worked in a soup kitchen himself) and fought the white slave market.

Basil was best known as an orator. His writings, though not recognized greatly in his lifetime, rightly place him among the great teachers of the Church. Seventy-two years after his death the Council of Chalcedon described him as "the great Basil, minister of grace who has expounded the truth to the whole earth."

COMMENT: As the French say, "The more things change, the more they remain the same." Basil faced the same problems as modern Christians. Sainthood meant trying to preserve the spirit of Christ in such perplexing and painful problems as reform, organization, fighting for the poor, maintaining balance and peace in misunderstanding.

QUOTE: St. Basil said: "The bread which you do not use is the bread of the hungry; the garment hanging in your wardrobe is the garment of him who is naked; the shoes that you do not wear are the shoes of the one who is barefoot; the money that you keep locked away is the money of the poor; the acts of charity that you do not perform are so many injustices that you commit."

Gregory Nazianzen (329-390)

Gregory gladly accepted his friend Basil's invitation to join him in a newly founded monastery after his baptism at 30. The solitude was broken when his father, a bishop, needed help in his diocese and estate. Gregory, it seems, was ordained priest practically by force, and only reluctantly accepted the responsibility. He was skillful in avoiding a schism that threatened because his own father made compromises with Arianism. At 41, he was chosen suffragan bishop of Caesarea and at once came into conflict with Valens, the emperor, who was supporting the Arians. An unfortunate by-product of the battle was the cooling of the friendship of two saints. Basil, his archbishop, sent him to a miserable and unhealthy town on the border of unjustly-created divisions in his diocese. Basil reproached Gregory for not going to his see.

When protection for Arianism ended with the death of Valens, Gregory was called to rebuild the faith in the great see of Constantinople which had been under Arian teachers for three decades. Retiring and sensitive, he dreaded being drawn into the whirlpool of corruption and violence. He first stayed at a friend's home, which became the only orthodox church in the city. In such surroundings, he began giving the great sermons on the Trinity for which he is famous. In time, he did rebuild the faith in the city, but at the cost of great suffering, slander, insults and even personal violence. An interloper even tried to take over his bishopric.

His last days were spent in solitude and austerity. He wrote religious poetry, some of it autobiographical, of great depth and beauty. He was acclaimed simply as "the Theologian."

COMMENT: It may be small comfort, but the present turmoil of change in the church is a mild storm compared to the devastation caused by the Arian heresy, a trauma the Church has never forgotten. Christ did not promise the kind of peace we would love to have — no problems, no opposition, no pain. In one way or another, holiness is always the way of the cross.

QUOTE: "God accepts our desires as though they were of great value. He longs ardently for us to desire and love him. He accepts our petitions for benefits as though we were doing him a favor. His joy in giving is greater than ours in receiving. So let us not be apathetic in our asking, nor set too narrow bounds to our requests; nor ask for frivolous things unworthy of God's greatness."

BLESSED ELIZABETH ANN SETON

(1774-1821)

Mother Seton is one of the keystones of the American Catholic Church. She founded the first native American religious community for women, the Sisters of Charity, opened the first American parish school and established the first American Catholic orphanage. All this she did in the span of 46 years while raising her five children.

Elizabeth Ann Bayley Seton is a true daughter of the American Revolution, born August 28, 1774, just two years before the Declaration of Independence. By birth and marriage, she was linked to the first families of New York and enjoyed the fruits of high society. Reared a staunch Episcopalian by her mother and stepmother, she learned the value of prayer, Scripture and a nightly examination of conscience. Her father, Dr. Richard Bayley, did not have much use for Churches but was a great humanitarian, teaching his daughter to love and serve others.

The early deaths of her mother in 1777 and her baby sister in 1778 gave Elizabeth a feel for eternity and the temporariness of the pilgrim life on earth. Far from being brooding and sullen, she faced each new "holocaust," as she put it, with hopeful cheerfulness.

At 19, Elizabeth was the belle of New York and married a handsome, wealthy businessman, William Magee Seton. They had five children before his busi-

ness failed and he died of tuberculosis. At 30, Elizabeth was widowed, penniless, with five small children to support.

While in Italy with her dying husband, Elizabeth witnessed Catholicity in action through family friends. Three basic points led her to become a Catholic: belief in the Real Presence, devotion to the Blessed Mother and conviction that the Catholic Church led back to the Apostles and to Christ. Many of her family and friends rejected her when she became a Catholic in March, 1805.

To support her children, she opened a school in

Boston. From the beginning, her group followed the lines of a religious community, which was officially founded in 1809.

The thousand or more letters of Mother Seton reveal the development of her spiritual life from ordinary goodness to heroic sanctity. She suffered great trials of sickness, misunderstanding, the death of loved ones (her husband and two young daughters) and the heartache of a wayward son. She died January 4, 1821, and on March 17, 1963, Pope John XXIII proclaimed her the first American-born citizen to be beatified.

COMMENT: Elizabeth Seton had no extraordinary gifts. She was not a mystic or stigmatic. She did not prophesy or speak in tongues. She had two great devotions: abandonment to the will of God and an ardent love for the Blessed Sacrament. She wrote to a friend, Julia Scott, that she would prefer to exchange the world for a "cave or a desert." "But God has given me a great deal to do, and I have always and hope always to prefer his will to every wish of my own." Her brand of sanctity is open to all if we love God and do his will.

QUOTE: Elizabeth Seton told her fellow sisters, "The first end I propose in our daily work is to do the will of God; secondly, to do it in the manner he wills it; and thirdly, to do it because it is his will."

JOHN NEUMANN, bishop
(1811-1860)

Perhaps because the United States got a later start in the history of the world, it has relatively few canonized saints. Of the four who are honored, two are "Blessed," i.e., they have not received the full honor of canonization.

Blessed John Neumann was born in what is now Czechoslovakia. After studying in Prague, he came to New York at 25 and was ordained a priest. He did missionary work in New York until he was 29, when he joined the Redemptorists and became the first of this order to profess vows in the U.S. He continued missionary work in Maryland, Virginia and Ohio, where he became popular with the Germans.

At 41, as bishop of Philadelphia, he organized the parochial school system into a diocesan one, increasing the number of pupils almost twentyfold within a short time.

Gifted with outstanding organizing ability, he drew into the city many teaching orders of sisters and the Christian Brothers. During his brief assignment as vice provincial for the Redemptorists, he placed them in the forefront of the parochial movement.

Well-known for his holiness and learning, spiritual writing and preaching, on October 13, 1963, he became the first American bishop to be beatified.

COMMENT: Neumann took seriously Our Lord's words, "Go and teach all nations." From Christ he received his instructions and the power to carry them out. For Christ does not give a mission without supplying the means to accomplish it. The Father's gift in Christ to John Neumann was his exceptional organizing ability which he used to spread the Good News.

Today the Church is in dire need of men and women to continue in our times the teaching of the Good News. The obstacles and inconveniences are real and costly. Yet if Christians would approach Christ, he would supply the necessary talents to answer today's needs. The Spirit of Christ will continue his work through the instrumentality of generous Christians.

QUOTE: "Since every man of whatever race, condition, and age is endowed with the dignity of a person, he has an inalienable right to an education corresponding to his proper destiny and suited to his native talents, his sex, his cultural background and his ancestral heritage. At the same time, this education should pave the way to brotherly association with other peoples, so that genuine unity and peace on earth may be promoted. For a true education aims at the formation of the human person with respect to the good of those societies of which, as a man, he is a member, and in whose responsibilities, as an adult, he will share" (Vatican II, Education, 1).

RAYMOND OF PENYAFORT
(1175-1275)

Since Raymond lived into his hundredth year, he had a chance to do many things. As a member of the Spanish nobility, he had the resources and the education to get a good start in life.

By the time he was 20 he was teaching philosophy. In his early 30's he earned a doctorate in both canon and civil law. At 47 he became a Dominican. Pope Gregory IX called him to Rome to work for him and to be his confessor. One of the things the Pope asked him to do was to gather together all the decrees of Popes and Councils that had been made in the 80 years since a similar collection by Gratian. Raymond compiled five books called the "Decretals." They were looked upon as one of the best organized collections of Church law until the 1917 codification of canon law.

Earlier, Raymond had written for confessors a book of cases. It was called *Summa de casibus poenitentiae.* More than just a list of sins and penances, it discussed pertinent doctrines and laws of the Church that pertained to the problem or case brought to the confessor.

When Raymond was 60 he was appointed Archbishop of Tarragona, the capital of Aragon. He didn't like the honor at all and ended up getting sick and resigning in two years.

He didn't get to enjoy his peace long, however, because when he was 63 he was elected by his fellow

Dominicans to be the head of the whole order, the second man to follow St. Dominic himself. Raymond worked hard, visited on foot all the Dominicans, reorganized their constitutions and got through a provision that a Master General be allowed to resign. When the new constitutions were accepted, Raymond, then 65, resigned.

He still had 35 years to oppose heresy and work for the conversion of the Moors in Spain. He got St. Thomas Aquinas to write his work *Against the Gentiles.*

In his hundredth year the Lord let Raymond retire.

COMMENT: Raymond was a lawyer, a canonist. Legalism is one of the things that the Church tried to rid herself of at Vatican II. It is too great a preoccupation with the letter of the law to the neglect of the spirit and purpose of the law. The law can become an end in itself, so that the value the law was intended to promote is overlooked. But we must guard against going to the opposite extreme and seeing law as useless or something to be lightly regarded. Laws ideally state those things that are for the best interests of everyone and make sure the rights of all are safeguarded. From Raymond, we can learn a respect for law as a means of serving the common good.

QUOTE: "He who hates the law is without wisdom, and is tossed about like a boat in a storm," (Sirach, 33:2).

HILARY, bishop and doctor
(315?-368)

This staunch defender of the divinity of Christ was a gentle and courteous man, devoted to writing some of the greatest theology on the Trinity and was like his Master in being labeled a "disturber of the peace." In a very troubled period in the Church, his holiness was lived out in both scholarship and controversy.

Raised a pagan, he was converted to Christianity when he met his God of nature in the Scriptures. His wife was still living when he was chosen, against his will, to be the bishop of Poitiers in France. He was soon taken up with battling what became the scourge of the fourth century, Arianism, which denied the divinity of Christ.

The heresy spread rapidly. St. Jerome said "The world groaned and marveled to find that it was Arian." When the emperor Constantius ordered all the bishops of the West to sign a condemnation of Athanasius, the great defender of the faith in the East, Hilary refused and was banished from France to faroff Phrygia (the day would come when he would be called the "Athanasius of the West"). While in exile, writing, he was invited by some semi-Arians (hoping for reconciliation) to a council the emperor called to counteract the council of Niceas. But Hilary predictably defended the Church, and when he sought public debate with the heretical bishop who had exiled him, the Arians, dreading the meeting and its outcome, pleaded with the emperor to send this troublemaker back home. Hilary was welcomed by his people.

COMMENT: Christ said his coming would not bring "peace" but a sword. The Gospels offer no support for us if we fantasize about a sunlit holiness that knows no problems. Christ did *not* escape at the last moment, though he did live happily ever after . . . after a life of controversy, problems, pain and frustration. Hilary, like all saints, simply had more of the same.

STORY: This immovable defender of orthodoxy was very gentle in reconciling the bishops of France who, in fear or ignorance had accepted the Arian creed. And while he wrote a blistering indictment of the emperor for sponsoring heresy, he could also point out, calmly, that sometimes the difference between heretical and orthodox doctrines was in the words rather than the ideas. He counseled bishops of the West, therefore, to be reserved in their condemnation. And this, of course, won him new enemies.

January 17   *Memorial*

ANTHONY, abbot
(251-356)

The life of Anthony will remind many of the life of St. Francis of Assisi. At 20, he was so moved by the Gospel message, "Go sell what you have and give it to the poor," that he actually did just that with his rich inheritance. He is different from Francis in that most of his life was spent in solitude. He saw the world completely covered with snares, and gave the church and the world the witness of solitary asceticism, great personal mortification and prayer. But no saint is anti-social, and Anthony drew many people to himself for spiritual healing and guidance.

At 54, he responded to many requests and founded a sort of monastery of scattered cells. Again, like Francis there was great fear of "stately buildings and well-laden tables."

At 60, he hoped to be a martyr in the renewed Roman persecution of 311, fearlessly exposing himself to danger while giving moral and material support to those in prison.

At 88, he was fighting the Arian heresy, that massive trauma from which it took the Church centuries to recover. "The mule kicking over the altar" denied the divinity of Christ.

Anthony is associated in art with a T-shaped cross, a pig, and a book. The pig and the cross are symbols of his valiant warfare with the devil—the cross his constant means of power over evil spirits, the pig a symbol of the devil himself. The book recalls his preference for "the book of nature" over the printed word.

Anthony died in solitude at 105.

COMMENT: In an age that smiles at the notion of devils and angels, a man known for his power over evil spirits must at least make us pause. And in a day when people speak of life as a "rat race," a man who devotes his life to solitude and prayer points to an essential of the Christian life in all ages. His hermit life reminds us of the absoluteness of our break with sin and the totalness of our commitment to Christ. Even in God's good world there is another world whose false values constantly tempt us.

STORY: Lest we be misled by the awesomeness of Anthony's asceticism, we have a statement from his biographer that presses the meaning and result of all Christian life: "Strangers knew him from among his disciples by the joy on his face."

Even the great emperor Constantine wrote to him, asking for his prayers. Anthony told his friends, "Don't be surprised that the emperor writes to me—he's just another man, as I am. But be astounded that God should have written to us, and that he has spoken to us by his Son."

FABIAN, pope and martyr
(d. 250)

Fabian was a Roman layman who came into the city from his farm one day as clergy and people were preparing to elect a new Pope. Eusebius, a church historian, says a dove flew in and settled on the head of Fabian. This sign united the votes of clergy and laity and he was chosen unanimously.

He led the church for 14 years and died a martyr's death during the persecution of Decius in 250 A.D. St. Cyprian wrote to his successor that he was an "incomparable" man whose glory in death matched the holiness and purity of his life.

In the catacombs of St. Callistus, the stone that covered Fabian's grave may still be seen, broken into four pieces, bearing the Greek words, "Fabian, bishop, martyr."

COMMENT: We can go confidently into the future, and accept the change that growth demands, only if we have firm roots in the past, in a living tradition. A few pieces of stone in Rome are a reminder to us that we are the bearers of 20 centuries of a living tradition of faith and courage in living the life of Christ and showing it to the world. We have brothers and sisters who have "gone before us marked with the sign of faith" to light the way for us.

QUOTE: "The blood of the martyrs is the seed of the Church" (Tertullian).

SEBASTIAN, martyr
(257?-288?)

Nothing is historically certain about St. Sebastian except that he was a Roman martyr, and was venerated in Milan even in the time of St. Ambrose, and that he was buried on the Appian Way, probably near the present basilica of St. Sebastian. Devotion to him spread rapidly, and he is mentioned in several martyrologies as early as 350 A.D.

The *legend* of St. Sebastian is important in art, and there is a vast iconography. What scholars now agree is a pious fable has Sebastian as entering the Roman army only because in that position he could assist the martyrs without arousing suspicion. Finally he was found out, hailed before the Emperor Diocletian and delivered to Mauretianian archers to be shot to death. His body was pierced with arrows, and he was left for dead. But he was found still alive by those who came to bury him. He recovered, but refused to flee. One day he took up a position near where the emperor was to pass. He accosted the emperor, denouncing him for this cruelty to Christians. This time the sentence of death was carried out. Sebastian was beaten to death with clubs.

COMMENT: The fact that many of the early saints made such a tremendous impression on the church—awakening widespread devotion, great praise from the greatest writers of the Church—is proof of the heroism of their lives. As has been said, legends are by definition not true. Yet they may express the very substance of the faith and courage evident in the lives of these heroes and heroines of Christ.

STORY: Another legend describes Sebastian's effectiveness in bolstering the courage of those in prison. Two men under sentence of death seemed about to give in to their captors. Sebastian made such an impassioned exhortation to constancy that not only confirmed the two in their original convictions but won over many other prisoners in the jail. Again, this particular story may not be true. But it is true of the lives of all saints.

January 21   *Memorial*
AGNES, virgin and martyr
(d. 258?)

Almost nothing is known of this saint except that she was very young—12 or 13—when she was martyred in the last half of the third century. Various modes of death have been suggested—beheading, burning, strangling.

Legend has it she was a beautiful girl whom many young men wanted to marry. Among those she refused, one reported her to the authorities as being a Christian. She was arrested and confined to a house of prostitution. The legend continues that one who looked upon her lustfully lost his sight, and had it restored by her prayer. She was condemned, executed and buried near Rome in a catacomb that eventually was named after her. The daughter of Constantine built a basilica in her honor.

COMMENT: Like that of a modern Maria Goretti, the martyrdom of a virginal young girl made a deep impression on a society enslaved to a materialistic outlook. Like Agatha, who died in similar circumstances. Agnes is a symbol that holiness does not depend on length of years, experience or human effort. It is a gift God offers to all, one he can protect in the most fearful of circumstances.

QUOTE: "This is a virgin's birthday; let us follow the example of her chastity. It is a martyr's birthday; let us offer sacrifices; it is the birthday of holy Agnes: let men be filled with wonder, little ones with hope, married women with awe, and the unmarried with emulation. It seems to me that this child, holy beyond her years and courageous beyond human nature, received the name of Agnes (Greek: pure) not as an earthly designation but as a revelation from God of what she was to be" (from St. Ambrose's discourse on virginity).

January 22   *Optional*

VINCENT, deacon and martyr
(d.304)

When Jesus deliberately began his "journey" to death, Luke says that he "set his face" to go to Jerusalem. It is this quality of rocklife courage that distinguishes the martyrs.

Most of what we know about this saint comes from the poet Prudentius. His "acts" have been rather freely colored by the imagination of their compiler. But St. Augustine, in one of his sermons on

St. Vincent, speaks of having the acts of his martyrdom before him. We are at least sure of his name, his being a deacon, the place of his death and burial.

According to the story we have (and, as with some of the other early martyrs, the unusual devotion they inspired must have had a basis in a very heroic life), Vincent was ordained deacon by his friend St. Valerius at Saragossa in Spain. The Roman emperors had published their edicts against the clergy in 303, and the following year against the laity. Vincent and his bishop were imprisoned in Valencia. Hunger and torture failed to break them. Like the youths in the fiery furnace, they seemed to thrive on suffering.

Valerius was sent into exile, and Dacian now turned the full force of his fury on Vincent. Tortures that sound like those of World War II were tried. But their main effect was the progressive disintegration of Dacian himself. He had the torturers beaten because they failed.

Finally he suggested a compromise: would Vincent at least give up the sacred books to be burned according to the emperor's edict? He would not. Torture on the gridiron continued, the prisoner remaining courageous, the torturer losing control of himself. Vincent was thrown into a filthy prison cell — and converted the jailer. Dacian wept with rage, but strangely enough, ordered the prisoner to be given some rest.

Friends among the faithful came to visit him, but he was to have no earthly rest. When they finally settled him on a comfortable bed, he went to his eternal rest.

COMMENT: The martyrs are heroic examples of what God's power can do. It is humanly impossible, we realize, for a man to go through tortures such as Vincent had and remain faithful. But it is equally true that by human power alone no one can remain faithful even *without* torture or suffering. God does not come to our rescue at isolated, "special" moments. He is supporting us all the time. He is like the ocean: supporting the super-crusiers as well as children's toy boats.

QUOTE: "Wherever it was that Christians were put to death, their executions did not bear the semblance of a triumph. Exteriorly they did not differ in the least from the executions of common criminals. But the moral grandeur of a martyr is essentially the same, whether he preserved his constancy in the arena before thousands of raving spectators or whether he perfected his martyrdom forsaken by all upon a pitiless flayer's field" (*The Roman Catacombs*, by Hertling-Kirschbaum).

January 24   *Memorial*

FRANCIS DE SALES,
bishop and doctor
(1567-1622)

Francis was destined by his father to be a lawyer so that he could eventually take his place as a senator from the Province of Savoy in France. For this reason he was sent to Padua to study law. After receiving his doctorate, he returned home, and, in due time, told his parents he wished to enter the priesthood. His father strongly opposed Francis in this, and only after much patient persuasiveness on the part of the gentle Francis did he finally consent. Francis was ordained and elected Provost of the Diocese of Geneva, then a center for the heretical Calvinists. Francis set out to convert them, especially in the district of Chablais. By preaching and distributing the little pamphlets he wrote to explain true Catholic doctrine he had remarkable success.

At 35 he became bishop of Geneva. While administering his diocese he continued to preach, hear confessions, and catechize the children. His gentle character was a great asset in winning souls. He practiced his own axiom: "A spoonful of honey attracts more flies than a barrelful of vinegar."

Besides his two well-known books, *The Introduction to the Devout Life* and *A Treatise on the Love of God*, he wrote many pamphlets and carried on a vast correspondence. For his writings, he has been named patron of the Catholic Press. His writings, filled with his characteristic gentle spirit, are addressed to lay people. He wants to make them understand that they too are called to be saints. As he wrote in *The Introduction to the Devout Life:* "It is an error, or rather a heresy, to say devotion is incompatible with the life of a soldier, a tradesman, a prince, or a married woman . . . It has happened that many have lost perfection in the desert who had preserved it in the world."

In spite of his busy and comparatively short life, he had time to collaborate with another saint, Jane

Frances de Chantal, in the work of establishing the Sisters of the Visitation. These women were to practice the virtues exemplified in Mary's visit to Elizabeth: humility, piety and mutual charity. They at first engaged to a limited degree in works of mercy for the poor and the sick. Today, while some communities conduct schools, others live a strictly contemplative life.

COMMENT: Francis de Sales took seriously the words of Christ "Learn of me for I am meek and humble of heart." As he said himself, it took him 20 years to conquer his quick temper, but no one ever suspected he had such a problem, so overflowing with good nature and kindness was his usual manner of acting. His perennial meekness and sunny disposition won for him the title of "Gentleman Saint."

QUOTE: Francis tells us: "The person who possesses Christian meekness is affectionate and tender towards everyone; he is disposed to forgive and excuse the frailties of others; the goodness of his heart appears in a sweet affability that influences his words and actions, presents every object to his view in the most charitable and pleasing light."

January 25   *Feast*

CONVERSION OF PAUL, apostle

Paul's entire life can be explained in terms of one experience — his meeting with Jesus on the road to Damascus. In an instant, he saw that all the zeal of his dynamic personality was being wasted, like the

strength of a boxer swinging wildly. Perhaps he had
never seen Jesus, though he was only some years
older. But he had acquired a zealot's hatred of all
Jesus stood for, as he began to "harass the church.
He entered house after house, dragged men and
women out, and threw them in jail." Now he himself
was "entered," possessed, all his energy harnessed to
one goal — being a slave of Christ in the ministry of
reconciliation, an instrument to help others experience the one Savior.

One sentence determined his theology: "I am
Jesus, whom you are persecuting." Jesus was
mysteriously identified with people — the loving
group of people Saul had been running down like
criminals. Jesus, he saw, was the mysterious fulfill-
ment of all he had been blindly pursuing.

From then on, his only work was to "make every
man complete in Christ. For this I work and struggle, impelled by that energy of his which is so powerful a force within me." "Our preaching of the Gospel
proved not a matter of words for you but one of
power; it was carried out in the Holy Spirit and out
of complete conviction."

Paul's life became a tireless proclaiming and living out of the message of the Cross: the Christian
dies baptismally to sin and is buried with Christ; he
is dead to all that is sinful, and unredeemed in the
world. He is made into a new creature, already sharing Christ's victory and someday to rise from the
dead like him. Through this Risen Christ the Father
pours out the Spirit on him, making him completely
new.

So Paul's great message to the world was: You

are saved entirely by God, not by anything you can do. Saving faith is the gift of total, free, personal and loving commitment to Christ, a commitment that then bears fruit in more "works" than the Law could ever contemplate.

COMMENT: Paul is undoubtedly hard to understand. His style often reflects the rabbinical style of argument of his day, and often his thought skips on mountain tops while we plod below. But perhaps our problems are accentuated by the fact that so many beautiful jewels have become part everyday coin in our Christian language. For instance: Charity is patient is kind.

QUOTE: "Love is patient; love is kind. Love is not jealous, it does not put on airs, it is not snobbish. Love is never rude, it is not self-seeking, it is not prone to anger; neither does it brood over injuries. Love does not rejoice in what is wrong but rejoices with the truth. There is no limit to love's forbearance, to its trust, its hope, its power to endure" (I Cor. 13).

January 26   *Memorial*

TIMOTHY and TITUS, bishops

Timothy (d. 97?)

What we know from the New Testament of Timothy's life makes it sound like that of a modern harried bishop. He had the honor of being a fellow apostle with Paul, sharing both the privilege of preaching the Gospel and suffering for it by opposition and imprisonment.

Timothy had a Greek father and a Jewish mother named Eunice. Being the product of a "mixed" marriage, he was considered illegitimate by the Jews. It was his grandmother, Lois, who first became Christian. Timothy was a convert of Paul around the year 47 and later joined him in his apostolic work. He was with Paul at the founding of the Church at Corinth. During the 15 years he worked with Paul, he became one of his most faithful and trusted friends. He was sent on difficult missions by Paul — often in the face of great disturbance in Churches Paul had founded.

Timothy was with Paul in Rome during the latter's house arrest. At some period Timothy himself was in prison (Hebrews 12:32). Paul installed him as his representative at the church of Ephesus.

Timothy was comparatively young for the work he was doing. ("Let no one look down on you because of your youth," Paul writes). Several references seem to indicate that he was timid. And one of Paul's frequently quoted lines was addressed to him: "Stop drinking water only. Take a little wine for the good of your stomach, and because of your frequent illnesses."

COMMENT: Nostalgia for the good old days in the Church — especially the early Church — should not blind us to the fact that the servants have never been greater than the Master. Their holiness was lived out in day to day perplexities, sufferings and apparent failure. The world is not saved by what we do, but by what God does through the life he creates in us.

QUOTE: Paul writes, in his second Letter to Timothy, 1:6-8: "I remind you to stir into flame the gift of God bestowed when my hands were laid on you. The Spirit God has given us is no cowardly spirit, but rather one that makes us strong, loving and wise. Therefore never be ashamed of your testimony to our Lord, nor of me, a prisoner for his sake; but with the strength that comes from God bear your share of the hardship which the gospel entails."

TITUS, bishop (d.94?)

Titus has the distinction of being a close friend and disciple of Paul as well as a fellow missionary. He was a Greek, apparently from Antioch. In spite of his being a Gentile, Paul would not let him be forced to undergo circumcision at Jerusalem. Titus is seen as a peace-maker, administrator, great friend. Paul's second letter to Corinth affords an insight into the depth of his friendship with Titus, and the great fellowship they had in preaching the Gospel. Paul writes, "When I came to Troas . . . I was inwardly troubled because I did not find my brother Titus there. So I said goodbye to them and went off to Macedonia . . . When I arrived I was restless and exhausted. I was under all kinds of stress — quarrels with others and fears within myself. But God, who gives heart to those who are low in spirit, gave me strength with the arrival of Titus." When Paul was having trouble with the community at Corinth, Titus was the bearer of his "severe letter." Titus "took no advantage of them" and was successful in smoothing things out. Paul writes he was strengthened not only by the arrival of Titus but also "by the reinforcement Titus has already received from you — for he reported your longing, your grief, and your ardent concern for me, so that my joy is greater still . . . His heart embraces you with an expanding love as he recalls the obedience you showed to God when you received him in fear and trembling."

In the Letter to Titus, he is seen to be administrator of the Christian community on the island of Crete, charged with organizing it, correcting abuses and appointing presbyter-bishops.

COMMENT: In Titus we get another glimpse of life in the early Church: great zeal in the apostolate, great communion in Christ, great friendship. Yet always there is the problem of human nature and the unglamorous details of daily life, the need for charity and patience in "quarrels with others, fears within myself," as Paul says. Through it all, the love of Christ sustained them. At the end of his letter to Titus, Paul says that when the temporary substitute comes, "hurry to me."

QUOTE: "When the kindness and love of God our Savior appeared, he saved us; not because of any righteous deeds we had done, but because of his mercy. He saved us through the baptism of new birth and renewal by the Holy Spirit. This Spirit he lavished on us through Jesus Christ our Savior, that we might be justified by his grace and become heirs, in hope, of eternal life. You can depend on this to be true" (Titus 3:4-8).

ANGELA MERICI, virgin
(1470?-1540)

Angela has the double distinction of founding the first teaching order of women in the church and what is now called a "secular institute" of religious women.

As a young woman she became a member of the Third Order of St. Francis, and lived a life of great austerity, wishing, like St. Francis, to own nothing, not even a bed. Early in life she was appalled at the ignorance among poorer children, whose parents could not or would not teach them the elements of religion. Angela's charming manner and good looks complemented her natural qualities of leadership. Others joined her in giving regular instruction to the little girls of their neighborhood.

She was invited to live with a family in Brescia (where, she has been told in a vision, she would one day found a religious community). Her work continued and became well known. She became the center of a group of people with similar ideals.

She eagerly took the opportunity for a trip to the Holy Land. When they had gotten as far as Crete, she was struck with blindness. Her friends wanted to return home, but she insisted on going through with the pilgrimage, and visited the sacred shrines with as much devotion and enthusiasm as if she had her sight. On the way back, while praying before a crucifix, her sight was restored at the same place where it had been lost.

At 57, she organized a group of 12 girls to help her in catechetical work. Four years later the group had increased to 28. She formed them into the Company of St. Ursula (patroness of medieval universities and venerated as a leader of women) for the purposes of re-Christianizing family life through solid Christian education of future wives and mothers. The members continued to live at home, had no special habit and took no formal vows, though the early rule prescribed the practice of virginity, poverty and obedience. The ideas of a teaching order of women was new, and took time to develop. The community thus existed as a "secular institute" until some years after Angela's death.

COMMENT: As with so many saints, history is mostly concerned with their activities. But we must always presume deep Christian faith and love in one whose courage lasts a lifetime, and who can take bold new steps when human need demands.

QUOTE: In a time when change is problematic to many, it may be helpful to recall a statement this great leader made to her sisters: "If according to times and needs you should be obliged to make fresh rules and change certain things, do it with prudence and good advice."

THOMAS AQUINAS, priest and doctor
(1225-1274)

By universal consent Thomas Aquinas is the preeminent spokesman of the Catholic tradition of reason and of divine revelation. He is one of the great teachers of the medieval Catholic Church, honored with the titles Doctor of the Church and Angelic Doctor.

At five he was given to the Benedictine monastery at Monte Cassino in his parents' hopes that he would choose that way of life and later become abbot. In 1239 he was sent to Naples to complete his studies. It was here that he was first attracted to Aristotle's philosophy.

By 1243, Thomas abandoned his family's plans for him and joined the Dominicans much to his mother's dismay. On her order, Thomas was captured by his brother and kept at home for over a year.

Once free, he went to Paris and then to Cologne, where he finished his studies with Albert the Great. He held two professorships at Paris, lived at the court of Pope Urban IV, directed the Dominican school at Rome and Viterbo, combated adversaries of the Mendicants and Averroists and argued with some Franciscans about Aristotelianism.

His greatest contribution to the Catholic Church is his writings. The unity, harmony and continuity of faith and reason, of revealed and natural human knowledge, pervades his writings. One might expect

Thomas, as a man of the Gospel, to be an ardent defender of revealed truth. But he was broad enough, deep enough, to see the whole natural order as coming from God the Creator, and to see reason as a divine gift to be highly cherished.

The "Summa Theologica," his last and, unfortunately, uncompleted work, deals with the whole of Catholic theology. He stopped work on it after celebrating Mass on Dec. 6, 1273. When asked why he stopped writing, he replied, "I cannot go on . . . All that I have written seems to me like so much straw compared to what I have seen and what has been revealed to me." He died March 7, 1274.

COMMENT: We can look to Thomas Aquinas as a towering example of Catholicism in the sense of broadness, universality, and inclusiveness. We should be determined anew to exercise the divine gift of reason in us, our power to know, learn and understand. At the same time we should thank God for the gift of his revelation, especially in Jesus Christ.

QUOTE: "Hence we must say that for the knowledge of any truth whatsoever man needs divine help, that the intellect may be moved by God to its act. But he does not need a new light added to his natural light, in order to know the truth in all things, but only in some that surpasses his natural knowledge" (Thomas Aquinas, *Summa Theologica*, 1-2, 109, 1).

JOHN BOSCO, priest
(1815-1888)

John Bosco's theory of education could well be used in today's schools. It was a preventive system, rejecting corporal punishment and placing students in surroundings removed from the likelihood of committing sin. He advocated frequent reception of the sacraments of Penance and Holy Communion. He combined catechetical training and fatherly guidance, seeking to unite the spiritual life with one's work, study and play.

Encouraged during his youth to become a priest so he could work with young boys, John was ordained in 1841. His service to youths started when he met a poor orphan and instructed him in preparation for receiving Holy Communion. He then gathered young apprentices and taught them catechism.

After serving as chaplain in a hospice for working girls, John opened the Oratory of St. Francis de Sales, for boys. Several wealthy and powerful patrons contributed money so he was able to provide two workshops for the boys, shoemaking and tailoring.

By 1856, the institution had grown to 150 boys and had added a printing press for publication of religious and catechetical pamphlets. His interest in vocational education and publishing justify him as patron of young apprentices and Catholic publishers.

John's preaching fame spread and by 1850 he trained his own helpers because of difficulties in retaining young priests. In 1854 he and his followers informally banded together under St. Francis de Sales.

With Pope Pius IX's encouragement, John gathered 17 men and founded the Salesians in 1859. Their activity concentrated on education and mission work. Later, he organized a group of Salesian Sisters to assist girls.

COMMENT: John Bosco educated the whole person — body and soul united. He believed that Christ's love and our faith in that love should pervade everything we do — work, study, play. For John Bosco, being a Christian was a fulltime effort, not a once-a-week, Mass-on-Sunday experience. It is searching and finding God and Jesus in everything we do, letting their love lead us. Yet, John realized the importance of job-training and the self-worth and pride that comes with talent and ability so he trained his students in the trade crafts, too.

QUOTE: "Every education teaches a philosophy; if not by dogma then by suggestion, by implication, by atmosphere. Every part of that education has a connection with every other part. If it does not all combine to convey some general view of life, it is not education at all" (G.K. Chesterton, *The Common Man*).

BLASE, bishop and martyr
(d. 316)

We know more about the devotion to St. Blase by Christians around the world than we know about the saint himself. His feast is observed as a holy day in the Eastern Church. The Council of Oxford, in 1222, prohibited servile labor in England on Blase's feast day. The Germans and Slavs hold him in special honor and for decades most U.S. Catholics yearly sought the blessing of St. Blase for their throats.

We know that Bishop Blase was martyred in his episcopal city of Sebastea, Armenia, in 316. The *legendary* "acts" of St. Blase were written 400 years later. According to them Blase was a good bishop, working hard to encourage the spiritual and physical health of his people. Although the Edict of Toleration, 311, granting freedom of worship in the Roman Empire was already five years old, persecution still raged in Armenia. Blase was apparently forced to flee to the back country. There he lived as a hermit in solitude and prayer, but made friends with the wild animals. One day a group of hunters seeking wild animals for the amphitheater stumbled upon Blase's cave. They were first surprised and then frightened. The bishop was kneeling in prayer surrounded by patiently waiting wolves, lions and bears.

As the hunters hauled Blase off to prison, the legend has it, a mother came with her young son who had a fish bone lodged in his throat. At Blase's command the child was able to cough up the bone.

Agricolaus, governor of Cappadocia, tried to persuade Blase to sacrifice to pagan idols. The first time he refused, he was beaten. The next time he was suspended from a tree and his flesh torn with iron combs or rakes. (English wool combers, who used similar iron combs, took Blase as their patron. They could easily appreciate the agony the saint underwent). Finally he was beheaded.

COMMENT: Four centuries give ample opportunity for fiction to creep in with fact. Who can be sure how accurate Blase's biographer was? But biographical details are not essential. Blase is seen as one more example of the power those have who give themselves entirely to Jesus. As Jesus told his apostles at the Last Supper, "If you live in me and my words stay part of you, you may ask what you will — it will be done for you" (John 15:7). With faith we can follow the lead of the Church in asking for Blase's protection.

QUOTE: "Through the intercession of St. Blase, bishop and martyr, may God deliver you from ailments of the throat and from every other evil. In the name of the Father, and of the Son and of the Holy Spirit" (Blessing of St. Blase).

ANSGAR, bishop
(801-865)

The "Apostle of the North" (Scandinavia) had enough frustrations to become a saint — and he did. He became a Benedictine at Corbie, where he had been educated. Three years later, when the king of Denmark became a convert, he went to that country for three years of missionary work, without noticeable success. Sweden asked for Christian missionaries, and Ansgar went there, suffering capture by pirates and other hardships on the way. Less than two years later he was recalled, to become abbot of Corvey and bishop of Hamburg. The Pope made him legate for the Scandinavian missions. Funds for the northern apostolate stopped with the emperor Louis' death. After 13 years' work in Hamburg, Ansgar saw it burned to the ground by invading Northmen; Sweden and Denmark returned to paganism.

He directed new apostolic activities in the North, himself traveling to Denmark and being instrumental in the conversion of another king. By the strange device of casting lots, the King of Sweden allowed the Christian missionaries to return.

Ansgar's biographers remark that he was an extraordinary preacher, a humble and ascetical priest. He was devoted to the poor and the sick, imitating the Lord in washing their feet and waiting on them at table. He died peacefully at Bremen, Germany, without achieving his wish to be a martyr.

Sweden became pagan again after his death, and

remained so until the coming of missionaries two centuries later.

COMMENT: History records what men do, rather than what they are. Yet the courage and perseverance of men like Ansgar can only come from a solid base of union with the original courageous and persevering Missionary. Ansgar's life is another reminder that God writes straight with crooked lines. Christ takes care of the effects of the apostolate in his own way; he is first concerned about the purity of the apostle himself.

STORY: One of his followers was bragging about all the miracles the saint had wrought. Ansgar rebuked him by saying "If I were worthy of such a favor from my God, I would ask that he grant me this one miracle: that by his grace he would make of me a good man."

February 5   *Memorial*

AGATHA, virgin and martyr
(d. 251?)

As in the case of Agnes, another virgin-martyr of the early church, almost nothing is historically certain about this saint except that she was martyred in Sicily during the persecution of the Roman emperor Decius in 251.

Legend has it Agatha, like Agnes, was arrested as a Christian, tortured and sent to a house of prostitution to be mistreated. She was preserved from being violated, and was later put to death.

She is claimed as the patroness of both Palermo

and Catania. The year after her death, the stilling of an eruption of Mt. Etna was attributed to her intercession. As a result, apparently, people continued to ask her prayers for protection against fire.

COMMENT: The scientific modern mind winces at the thought of a volcano's might being contained by God because of the prayers of a Sicilian girl. Still less welcome, probably, is the notion of that saint being the patroness of such varied professions as those of foundrymen, nurses, miners and Alpine guides. Yet, in our historical precision, have we lost an essential human quality of wonder and poetry, and even our belief that we come to God by helping each other, both in action and prayer?

QUOTE: When Agatha was arrested, the legend says, she prayed: "Jesus Christ, Lord of all things! You see my heart, you know my desires. Possess all that I am — you alone. I am your sheep; make me worthy to overcome the devil." And in prison: "Lord, my creator, you have protected me since I was in the cradle. You have taken me from the love of the world and given me patience to suffer. Now receive my spirit."

February 5   *Memorial*

PAUL MIKI and COMPANIONS, martyrs
(d. 1597)

Nagasaki, Japan, is familiar to Americans as the city on which the second atomic bomb was dropped, killing hundreds of thousands. Three and a half centuries before, 26 martyrs of Japan were crucified on a hill, now known as the Holy Mountain, overlooking Nagasaki. Among them were priests, brothers and laymen, Franciscans, Jesuits and members of the Third Order of St. Francis; there were catechists, doctors, simple artisans and servants; old men and innocent children; all united in a common faith and love for Jesus and his Church.

Brother Paul Miki, a Jesuit and a native of Japan, has become the best known among the martyrs of Japan. While hanging upon a cross Paul Miki preached to the people gathered for the execution: "The sentence of judgement says these men came to Japan from the Philippines, but I did not come from any other country. I am a true Japanese. The only reason for my being killed is that I have taught the doctrine of Christ. I certainly did teach the doctrine of Christ. I thank God it is for this reason I die. I believe that I am telling only the truth before I die. I know you believe me and I want to say to you all once again: Ask Christ to help you to become happy. I obey Christ. After Christ's example I forgive my persecutors. I do not hate them. I ask God to have pity on all, and I hope my blood will fall on my fellow men as a fruitful rain."

When missionaries returned to Japan in the 1860's they at first found no trace of Christianity. But after establishing themselves they found that thousands of Christians lived around Nagasaki and that they had secretly preserved the faith. Beatified already in 1627, the martyrs of Japan were finally canonized in 1862.

COMMENT: Today a new era has come for the Church in Japan. Although the number of Catholics is not large, the Church is respected and has total religious freedom. The spread of Christianity in the Far East is slow and difficult. Faith and zeal such as that of the 26 Martyrs are needed today as much as in 1597.

QUOTE: "Since Jesus, the Son of God, manifested his charity by laying down his life for us, no one has greater love than he who lays down his life for Christ and his brothers. From the earliest times, then, some Christians have been called upon — and some will always be called upon—to give this supreme testimony of love to all men, but especially to persecutors. The Church, therefore, considers martyrdom as an exceptional gift and as the highest proof of love.

Though few are presented with such an opportunity, nevertheless, all must be prepared to confess Christ before men, and to follow him along the way of the cross through the persecutions which the Church will never fail to suffer" (Vatican II, Constitution on the Church, 42).

February 8   *Optional*

JEROME EMILIANI
(1481-1537)

A careless and irreligious soldier for the city-state of Venice, Jerome was captured in a skirmish at an outpost town and chained in a dungeon. In prison

Jerome had a lot of time to think, and he gradually learned how to pray. When he escaped, he returned to Venice where he took charge of the education of his nephews—and began his own studies for the priesthood.

In the years after his ordination events again called Jerome to a decision and a new life-style. Plague and famine swept northern Italy. Jerome began caring for the sick and feeding the hungry at his own expense. In his service to the sick and the poor he soon resolved to devote himself and his property solely to others, particularly to abandoned children. He founded three orphanages, a shelter for penitent prostitutes and a hospital.

Around 1532 Jerome and two other priests established a congregation dedicated to the care of orphans and the education of youth. Jerome died in 1537 from a disease he caught while tending the sick. In 1928 Pius XI named him the patron of orphans and abandoned children.

COMMENT: Very often in our lives it seems to take some kind of "imprisonment" to free us from the shackles of our self-centeredness. When we're "caught" in some situation we don't want to be in, we finally come to know the liberating power of Another. Only then can we become an Another for "the imprisoned" and "the orphaned" all around us.

QUOTE: "The father of orphans and the defender of widows is God in his holy dwelling. God gives a home to the forsaken; he leads forth prisoners to prosperity; only rebels remain in parched land. (Psalm 68) . . . We should not forget the growing number of persons who are often abandoned by their families and by the community: the old, orphans, the sick and all kinds of people who are rejected . . . We must be prepared to take on new functions and new duties in every sector of human activity and especially in the sector of world society, if justice is really to be put into practice. Our action is to be directed above all at those men and nations which because of various forms of oppression and because of the present character of our society are silent, indeed voiceless, victims of injustice" ("Justice in the World," 1971 World Synod of Bishops).

SCHOLASTICA, virgin
(480-542?)

Twins often share the same interests and ideas with an equal intensity. Therefore, it is no surprise that Scholastica and her twin brother, Benedict, both established religious communities within a few miles from each other.

Born in 480 of wealthy parents, Scholastica and Benedict were brought up together until he left for Rome to continue his studies.

Little is known of Scholastica's early life. She founded a religious community for women near Monte Cassino at Plombariola, five miles from where her brother governed a monastery.

The twins visited each other once a year in a farmhouse because Scholastica was not permitted inside the monastery. They spent these times discussing spiritual matters.

According to the *Dialogues of St. Gregory the Great,* the brother and sister spent their last day together in prayer and conversation. Scholastica sensed her death was close at hand and she begged Benedict to stay with her until the next day.

He refused her request because he did not want to spend a night outside the monastery, thus breaking his own rule. Scholastica asked God to let her brother remain and a severe thunderstorm broke out, preventing Benedict and his monks from returning to the abbey.

Benedict cried out, "God forgive you, Sister. What have you done?" Scholastica replied, "I asked a favor of you and you refused. I asked it of God and he granted it."

Brother and sister parted the next morning after their long discussion. Three days later, Benedict was praying in his monastery and saw the soul of his sister rising heavenward in the form of a white dove. Benedict then announced the death of his sister to the monks and later buried her in the tomb he had prepared for himself.

COMMENT: Scholastica and Benedict gave themselves totally to God and gave top priority to deepening their friendship with him through prayer. They sacrificed some of the opportunities they would have had to get together as brother and sister to better fufill their vocation to the religious life. In coming closer to Christ, however, they found they were also closer to each other. In joining a religious community, they did not forget or forsake their family but rather found more brothers and sisters.

QUOTE: "All religious have the duty, each according to his proper vocation, of cooperating zealously and diligently in building up and increasing the whole Mystical Body of Christ and for the good of the particular churches . . . It is their duty to foster these objectives primarily by means of prayer, works of penance, and the example of their own life" (Vatican II, Bishops, 33).

February 14   *Memorial*

CYRIL, monk (d. 869)
and METHODIUS, bishop (d. 884)

Because their father was an officer in a part of Greece inhabited by many Slavs, these two Greek brothers ultimately became missionaries, teachers and patrons of the Slavic peoples.

After a brilliant course of studies, Cyril (called Constantine until he became a monk shortly before his death) refused the governorship of a district such as his brother had accepted among the Slavic-speaking population. He withdrew to a monastery where his brother Methodius had become a monk after some years in a governmental post.

A decisive change in their lives occurred when the Duke of Moravia (present-day Moravia and Slovakia) asked the Eastern Emperor Michael for political independence from German rule and ecclesiastical autonomy (having their own clergy and liturgy). Cyril and Methodius undertook the missionary task.

Cyril's first work was to invent an alphabet,

probably still used in Yugoslavian liturgy. His followers probably formed the Cyrillic alphabet (e.g., modern Russian) from Greek capital letters. Together they translated the Gospels, the Psalter, Paul and the liturgical books into Slavic, and composed a Slavic liturgy, highly irregular then.

That, and their free use of the vernacular in preaching, led to opposition from the German clergy. The bishop refused to consecrate Slavic bishops and priests, and Cyril was forced to appeal to Rome. On the visit to Rome, they had the joy of seeing their new liturgy approved by Pope Adrian II. Cyril, long an invalid, died in Rome 50 days after taking the monastic habit.

Methodius continued mission work for 16 more years. He was papal legate for all the Slavic peoples, consecrated bishop and then given an ancient see (in present Yugoslavia). When much of their former territory was removed from their jurisdiction, the Bavarian bishop retaliated with a violent storm of accusation against Methodius. As a result, Emperor Louis the German exiled Methodius for three years. Pope John VIII secured his release.

The Frankish clergy, still smarting, continued their accusations, and Methodius had to go to Rome to defend himself against charges of heresy and uphold his use of the Slavic liturgy. He was again vindicated.

Legend has it that in a feverish period of activity, Methodius translated the whole Bible into Slavic in eight months. He died on Tuesday of Holy Week, surrounded by his disciples, in his cathedral church.

Opposition continued after his death, and the

work of the brothers in Moravia was brought to an end, and their disciples scattered. But the expulsions had the beneficial effect of spreading the spiritual, liturgical and cultural work of the brothers to Bulgaria, Bohemia and southern Poland. Patrons of Moravia, and specially venerated by Catholic Czechs, Slovaks, Croations, Orthodox Serbians and Bulgarians, Cyril and Methodius are eminently fitted to guard the long-desired unity of East and West.

COMMENT: Holiness means reacting to human life with God's love: human life *as it is,* criss-crossed with the political and the cultural, the beautiful and the ugly, the selfish and the saintly. For Cyril and Methodius much of their daily cross had to do with a problem familiar to us today: the language of the liturgy. They are not saints because they got the liturgy into Slavic, but because they did so with the courage and humility of Christ.

QUOTE: "Even in the liturgy, the Church has no wish to impose a rigid uniformity in matters which do not involve the faith or the good of the whole community. Rather she respects and fosters the spiritual adornments and gifts of the various races and peoples . . . Provided that the substantial unity of the Roman rite is maintained, the revision of liturgical books should allow for legitimate variations and adaptations to different groups, religions, and peoples, especially in mission lands" (Vatican II, Liturgy, 37,38).

SEVEN FOUNDERS OF THE
ORDER OF SERVITES (13th cent.)

Can you imagine seven prominent men of Boston or San Francisco banding together, leaving their homes and professions, and going into solitude for a life directly given to God? That is what happened in the cultured and prosperous city of Florence in the middle of the 13th century. The city was torn with political strife as well as the heresy of the Cathari. Morals were low, and religion seemed meaningless.

In 1240 seven noblemen of Florence mutually decided to withdraw from the city to a solitary place for prayer and direct service of God. Their initial difficulty was providing for their dependents, since two were still married and two were widowers.

Their aim was to lead a life of penance and prayer, but they soon found themselves disturbed by constant visitors from Florence. They next withdrew to the deserted slopes of Monte Senario.

In 1244, under the direction of St. Peter of Verona, O.P., this small group adopted a religious habit similar to the Dominican habit, choosing to live under the rule of St. Augustine and adopting the name of the Servants of Mary. The new order took a form more like that of the mendicant friars than that of the older monastic orders.

Members of the community came to the United States from Austria in 1852 and settled in New York and later in Philadelphia. The two American provinces have developed from the foundation made by Father Austin Morini in 1870 at St. Charles

Church, Menasha, Wisconsin.

Community members combined monastic life and active ministry. In the monastery, they lead a life of prayer, work and silence while in the active apostolate they engage in parochial work, teaching, preaching and other ministerial activities.

COMMENT: The time in which the seven servite founders lived is very easily comparable to the situation in which we find ourselves today. It is "the best of times and the worst of times," as Dickens said. Some, perhaps many, feel called to a "counter-culture" life, even in religion. All of us are faced in a new and urgent way with the challenge to make our lives *decisively* centered in Christ.

QUOTE: "Let all religious therefore spread throughout the whole world the good news of Christ by the integrity of their faith, their love for God and neighbor, their devotion to the Cross and their hope of future glory . . . Thus, too, with the prayerful aid of that most loving Virgin Mary, God's Mother, 'Whose life is a rule of life for all,' religious communities will experience a daily growth in numbers, and will yield a richer harvest of fruits that bring salvation" (Vatican II, Religious Life, 25).

February 21   *Optional*

PETER DAMIAN, bishop and doctor
(1007-1072)

Maybe because he was orphaned and had been treated shabbily by one of his brothers, Peter Damian was very good to the poor. It was the ordinary thing for him to have a poor person or two with him at table and he liked to personally minister to their needs.

Peter had himself escaped poverty and the neglect of his own brother when his other brother, who was archpriest of Ravenna, took him under his wing. He sent him to good schools, and Peter became a professor.

Already in these days Peter was very strict with himself. He wore a hair shirt under his clothes, fasted rigorously and spent many hours in prayer. Soon, he decided to leave his teaching and give himself completely to prayer with the Benedictines of the reform of St. Romuald at Fonte Avellana. They lived two monks to a hermitage. Peter was so eager to pray and slept so little that he soon suffered from severe insomnia. He found he had to use some prudence in taking care of himself. When he was not praying, he studied the Bible.

The abbot commanded that when he died Peter should succeed him. As abbot Peter founded five other hermitages. He encouraged his brothers in a life of prayer and solitude and wanted nothing more for himself. The Holy See periodically called on him; however, to be a peacemaker or troubleshooter between two abbeys in dispute or a clergyman or government official in some disagreement with Rome.

Finally, Pope Stephen IX made Peter the cardinal-bishop of Ostia. He worked hard to wipe out simony, and encouraged his priests to observe celibacy and urged even the diocesan clergy to live together and maintain scheduled prayer and religious observance. He wished to restore primitive discipline among religious and priests, warning against needless travel, violations of poverty and too comfortable living. He even wrote to the Bishop of Besancon complaining that the canons there sat down when they were singing the psalms in the Divine Office.

He wrote many letters. Some 170 are extant. We also have 53 of his sermons and seven lives, or biographies, that he wrote. He preferred examples and stories rather than theory in his writings. The liturgical offices he wrote are evidence of his talent as a stylist in Latin.

He asked often to be allowed to retire as cardinal-bishop of Ostia, and finally Alexander II consented. Peter was happy to become once again just a monk, but he was still called to serve as a papal legate. When returning from such an assignment in Ravenna, he was overcome by a fever. With the monks gathered around him saying the Divine Office, he died on February 22, 1072.

In 1828 he was declared a doctor of the Church.

COMMENT: Peter was a reformer and if he were alive today would no doubt have encouraged the renewal started by Vatican II. He would also have applauded the greater emphasis on prayer that is shown by the growing number of prayer meetings attended by priests, religious and lay men and women, as well as the special houses of prayer recently established by many religious communities. He may be an understanding patron for the reportedly 20 million insomniacs in the United States.

QUOTE: ". . . Let us faithfully transmit to posterity the example of virtue which we have received from our forefathers" (St. Peter Damian).

February 22   *Feast*

CHAIR OF PETER, apostle

This feast commemorates Christ's choosing Peter to sit in his place as the servant-authority of the whole Church. (See June 29)

After the "lost weekend" of pain, doubt and self-torment, Peter hears the good news. Angels at the tomb say to Magdalen, "He has risen! Go, tell his disciples and Peter." John relates that when he and Peter ran to the tomb, the younger outraced the older, then waited for him. Peter entered, saw the wrappings on the ground, the headpiece rolled up in a place by itself. John saw and believed. But he adds: "Remember, as yet they did not understand the Scripture that Jesus had to rise from the dead." They went home. There the slowly exploding, impossible idea became reality. Jesus appears to them, as they wait fearfully behind locked doors. "Peace be to you!" And they rejoiced.

The Pentecostal event completed Peter's experience of the Risen Christ. "They were all filled with the Holy Spirit" and began to express themselves in foreign tongues and make bold proclamation as the Spirit prompted them.

Now Peter can fulfill the task Jesus had given him: "And you, Peter, being converted, confirm your brothers." He is at once the spokesman for the

Twelve about their experience of the Holy Spirit; before the civil authorities who wished to quash their preaching; before the council of Jerusalem; for the community in the problem on Ananias and Sapphira. He is the first to preach the good news to the Gentiles. The healing power of Jesus in him is well attested: the raising of Tabitha from the dead, the cure of the crippled beggar. People carried the sick into the streets so that when Peter passed his shadow might fall on them.

Even a saint experiences difficulty in Christian living. When Peter stopped eating with Gentile converts because he did not want to wound the sensibilities of Christian Jews, Paul says, "I directly withstood him, because he was clearly in the wrong . . . . They were not being straightforward about the truth of the Gospel."

At the end of John's Gospel, Jesus says to Peter, "I tell you solemnly, as a young man you fastened your belt and went about as you pleased; but when you are older, you will stretch out your hands and another will tie you fast, and carry you off against your will." What he said indicated the sort of death by which Peter was to glorify God.

On Vatican Hill, in Rome, during the reign of Nero, Peter did glorify his Lord with a martyr's death, probably in the company of many Christians.

COMMENT: Peter described the Christian life, and therefore his own holiness and ours, in the first words of his letter: "We are chosen according to the foreknowledge of God the Father, consecrated by the Spirit to a life of obedience to Jesus Christ. . . . Praised be the God and Father of our Lord

Jesus Christ, who in his great mercy gave us new birth; a birth unto hope which draws its life from the resurrection of Jesus Christ from the dead; a birth to imperishable inheritance, incapable of fading or defilement."

STORY: This saintly man's life is perhaps best summed up at his meeting with Jesus after the resurrection. In the presence of the men he was to lead in imitation of his triple denial, Jesus asked him three times, "Simon, son of John, do you love me?" Peter answered, "Yes, Lord, you know that I love you. You know everything. You know well that I love you!"

February 23   *Memorial*
POLYCARP, bishop and martyr
(d. 156)

Polycarp, Bishop of Smyrna (modern Izmir, Turkey), disciple of St. John the Apostle and friend of St. Ignatius of Antioch was a revered Christian leader during the first half of the second century.

St. Ignatius, on his way to Rome to be martyred, visited Polycarp at Smyrna, and later at Troas, wrote him a personal letter. The Asia Minor Churches recognized Polycarp's leadership by choosing him as a representative to discuss with Pope Anicetus the date of the Easter celebration in Rome—quite a controversy in the early Church.

Only one of the many letters written by Polycarp has been preserved, his Letter to the Philippians (Church of Philippi, Macedonia).

At 86, Polycarp was led into the crowded Smyrna stadium to be burned alive and finally killed by a dagger. The centurion ordered the saint's body burned. The Acts of Polycarp's martyrdom are the earliest preserved, fully reliable account of a Christian martyr's death. He died in 156.

COMMENT: Polycarp was recognized as a Christian leader by all Asia Minor Christians—a strong fortress of faith and loyalty to Jesus Christ. His own strength emerged from his trust in God, even when events contradicted this trust. Living among pagans and under a government opposed to the new religion, he led and fed his flock. Like the Good Shepherd, he laid down his life for his sheep and kept them from more persecution in Smyrna. He summarized his trust in God just before he died: "Father . . . I bless Thee, for having made me worthy of the day and hour . . ." (*Martyrdom,* Ch. 14.).

QUOTE: "Stand fast, therefore, in this conduct and follow the example of the Lord, 'firm and unchangeable in faith, lovers of the brotherhood, loving each other, united in truth,' helping each other with the mildness of the Lord, despising no man" (Polycarp, *Letter to the Philippians,* Ch. 10).

March 4   *Optional*

CASIMIR
(1458-1483)

A teenaged conscientious objector is the patron saint of Poland and Lithuania. Casimir, born of kings and in line (third, among 13 children) to be a king himself, was filled with exceptional values and learning by a great teacher, John Dlugosz. Even his critics could not say that his conscientious objection indicated softness. Casimir lived, already as a teenager, a highly disciplined, even severe, life, sleeping on the ground, spending a great part of the night in prayer and dedicating himself to lifelong celibacy.

When nobles in Hungary became dissatisfied with their king, they prevailed upon Casimir's father, king of Poland, to send his son to take over the country. Casimir obeyed his father, as many young men over the centuries have obeyed their government. The army he was supposed to lead was clearly outnumbered by the "enemy"; some of his troops were deserting because they were not paid. At the advice of his officers, Casimir decided to return home. His father was irked at the failure of his plans, and confined the 15-year old son for three months. The lad made up his mind never again to become involved in the wars of his day, and no amount of persuasion could change his mind. He returned to prayer and study, maintaining his decision to remain celibate even under pressure to marry the emperor's daughter. He reigned briefly as King of Poland during his father's absence. He died of lung trouble at 23 while visiting Lithuania, of which he was also Grand Duke. He was buried in Vilna, Lithuania.

COMMENT: Poland and Lithuania have faded into the gray prison on the other side of the Iron Curtain. Despite repression, the Poles and Lithuanians remain firm in the faith which has become synonymous with their name. Their youthful patron offers them hope: peace is not won by war; sometimes a comfortable peace is not even won by virtue, but Christ's peace can penetrate even iron curtains.

STORY: Casimir had great love of the Mother of God; in particular he loved the great Marian Latin hymn, "Omni die dic Mariae" (translated, not literally, as "Daily, daily, sing to Mary"). He asked that a copy of it be buried with him.

March 7   *Memorial*
PERPETUA and FELICITY, martyrs
(d. 203?)

"When my father in his affection for me was trying to turn me from my purpose by arguments and thus weaken my faith, I said to him, 'Do you see this vessel—waterpot or whatever it may be? Can it be called by any other name than what it is?' 'No,' he replied. 'So also I cannot call myself by any other name than what I am—a Christian.' "

So writes Perpetua, young, beautiful, well-educated, a noblewoman of Carthage, mother of an infant son and chronicler of the persecution of the Christians by the emperor Septimius Severus.

Despite threats of persecution and death, Perpetua, Felicity (a slavewoman and expectant mother), and three companions, Revocatus, Secundulus and Saturninus, refused to renounce their Christian faith. For their unwillingness, all were sent to the public games in the amphitheater. There, Perpetua and Felicity were beheaded, and the others killed by beasts.

Perpetua's mother was a Christian and her father a pagan. He continually pleaded with her to deny her faith. She refused and was imprisoned, at 22.

In her diary, Perpetua describes her period of captivity: "What a day of horror! Terrible heat, owing to the crowds! Rough treatment by the soldiers! To crown all, I was tormented with anxiety for my baby . . . . Such anxieties I suffered for many days, but I obtained leave for my baby to remain in the prison with me, and, being relieved of my trouble and anxiety for him, I at once recovered my health, and my prison became a palace to me and I would rather have been there than anywhere else."

Felicity gave birth to a girl a few days before the games commenced.

Perpetua's record of her trial and imprisonment ends the day before the games. "Of what was done in the games themselves, let him write who will." The diary was finished by an eyewitness.

COMMENT: Persecution for religious beliefs is not confined to Christians in ancient times. Consider Anne Frank, the Jewish girl who, with her family, was forced into hiding and later gassed to death by Hitler's Nazis during World War II. Anne, like Perpetua and Felicity, endured hardship and suffering and finally death because she committed herself to God. In her diary, Anne writes, "It's twice as hard for us young ones to hold our ground, and maintain our opinions, in a time when all ideals are being shattered and destroyed, when people are showing their worst side, and do not know whether to believe in truth and right and God."

QUOTE: Perpetua, unwilling to renounce Christianity, comforted her father in his grief over her decision, "It shall happen as God shall choose, for assuredly we depend not on our own power but on the power of God."

JOHN OF GOD, religious
(1495-1550)

Having given up active Christian belief while a soldier, John was 40 before the depth of his sinfulness began to dawn on him. He decided to give the rest of his life to God's service, and headed at once for Africa, where he hoped to free captive Christians, and possibly, be martyred.

He was soon advised that his desire for martyrdom was not spiritually well-based, and returned to Spain and the relatively prosaic activity of a religious goods store. Yet he was still not settled. Moved initially by a sermon of Blessed John of Avila, he one day engaged in a public beating of himself, begging mercy and wildly repenting for his past life.

Committed to a mental hospital for these actions, John was visited by Blessed John who advised him to be more actively involved in tending to the needs of others rather than in enduring personal hardships. John gained peace of heart, and shortly after left the hospital to begin work among the poor.

He established a house where he wisely tended to the needs of the sick-poor, at first doing his own begging. But, excited by the saint's great work and inspired by his devotion, many people began to back him up with money and provisions. Among them were the archbishop and marquis of Tarifa.

Behind John's outward acts of total concern and love for Christ's sick-poor, was a deep interior prayer life which was reflected in his spirit of humility. These qualities attracted helpers who, 20 years after John's death, formed the Brothers Hospitallers, now a world-wide religious order.

John became ill after 10 years of service but tried to disguise his ill health. He began to put the hospital's administrative work into order and appointed a leader for his helpers. He died under the care of a spiritual friend and admirer, Lady Anne Ossorio.

COMMENT: The utter humility of John of God which led to a totally selfless dedication to others, is most impressive. Here is a man who realized his nothingness in the face of God. The Lord blessed him with the gifts of prudence, patience, courage, enthusiasm and the ability to influence and inspire others. He saw that in his early life he had turned away from the Lord, and, moved to receive His mercy, John began his new commitment to love others, in openness to God's love.

STORY: The archbishop called John of God to him in response to a complaint that he was keeping tramps and immoral women in his hospital. In submission John fell on his knees and said: "The Son of Man came for sinners, and we are bound to seek their conversion. I am unfaithful to my vocation because I neglect this, but I confess that I know of no bad person in my hospital except myself alone, who am indeed unworthy to eat the bread of the poor." The archbishop could only trust in John's sincerity and humility, and dismissed him with deep respect.

FRANCES OF ROME, religious
(1384-1440)

Frances' life combines aspects of secular and religious life. A devoted and loving wife, she longed for a life style of prayer and service, so she organized a group of women to minister to the needs of Rome's poor.

Born of wealthy parents, Frances found herself attracted to the religious life during her youth. But her parents objected and a young nobleman was selected to be her husband.

As she became acquainted with her new relatives, Frances soon discovered that the wife of her husband's brother also wished to live a life of service and prayer. So the two, Frances and Vannozza, set out together — with their husbands' blessings — to help the poor.

Frances fell ill for a time, but this apparently only deepened her commitment to the suffering people she met. The years passed, and Frances gave birth to two sons and a daughter. With the new responsibilities of family life, the young mother

turned her attention more to the needs of her own household. The family flourished under Frances' care, but within a few years a great plague began to sweep across Italy. It struck Rome with devastating cruelty and left Frances' second son dead. In an effort to help alleviate some of the suffering, Frances used all her money and sold her possessions to buy whatever the sick might possibly need. When all the resources had been exhausted, Frances and Vannozza went door to door begging. Later, Frances' daughter died, and the saint opened a section of her house as a hospital.

Frances became more and more convinced that this way of life was so necessary for the world, and it was not long before she requested and was given permission to found a society of women bound by no vows. They simply offered themselves to God and to the service of the poor. Once the society was established, Frances chose not to live at the community residence, but rather at home with her husband. She did this for seven years, until her husband passed away, and then came to live the remainder of her life with the society — serving the poorest of the poor.

COMMENT: Looking at the exemplary life of fidelity to God and devotion to her fellow human beings which Frances of Rome was blessed to lead, one cannot help but be reminded of Mother Teresa of Calcutta today. Mother Teresa sees this same vision of loving Jesus Christ in prayer and also in the poor. The life of Frances of Rome calls each of us to look deeply for God in prayer, but to carry our devotion to Jesus living in the suffering of our world. Frances shows us that this life need not be restricted to those bound by vows.

QUOTE: In *Something Beautiful for God*, Mother Teresa says of the sisters in her community: "Let Christ radiate and live his life in her and through her in the slums. Let the poor seeing her be drawn to Christ and invite him to enter their homes and lives." Says Frances of Rome: "It is most laudable in a married woman to be devout, but she must never forget that she is a housewife. And sometimes she must leave God at the altar to find Him in her housekeeping" (Butler's *Lives of the Saints*).

PATRICK, bishop
(389?-461?)

Legends about Patrick abound; but truth is best served by our seeing two solid qualities in him: he was humble and he was courageous. The determination to accept suffering and success with equal indifference guided the life of God's instrument for winning most of Ireland for Christ.

Details of his life are uncertain. Patrick's birthplace is said to be either Dunbarton, Scotland or Cumberland, England. He called himself both a Roman and a Briton. At 16, he and a large number of his father's slaves and vassals were captured by Irish raiders and sold as slaves in Ireland. Forced to work as a shepherd, he suffered greatly from hunger and cold.

After six years, Patrick escaped, probably to France, and later returned to Britain at the age of 22. His captivity had meant spiritual conversion. He may have studied at Lerins, off the French coast; he spent 15 years at Auxerre, and was consecrated bishop at the age of 43. His great desire was to proclaim the Good News to the Irish.

In a dream vision, it seemed "all the children of Ireland from their mothers' wombs, were stretching out their hands" to him. He understood the vision to be a call to do mission work in pagan Ireland. Despite opposition from those who felt his education had been defective, he was sent to carry out the task. He went to the west and north, where the faith had never been preached, obtained the protection of local kings, and made numerous converts.

Because of the island's pagan background, Patrick was emphatic in encouraging widows to remain chaste and young women to consecrate their virginity to Christ. He ordained many priests, divided the country into dioceses, held Church councils, founded several monasteries and continually urged his people to greater holiness in Christ.

He suffered much opposition from pagan druids, and was criticized in both England and Ireland for the way he conducted his mission.

In a relatively short time the island had deeply experienced the Christian spirit, and was prepared to send out missionaries whose efforts were greatly responsible for Christianizing Europe.

He was a man of action, with little inclination toward learning. He had a rocklike belief in his vocation, in the cause he had espoused.

One of the few certainly authentic writings is his *Confessio*, and above all an act of homage to God for having called Patrick, unworthy sinner, to the apostolate.

There is hope, rather than irony, in the fact that his burial place is said to be in strife-torn Ulster, in County Down.

COMMENT: What distinguishes Patrick is the durability of his efforts. When one considers the state of Ireland when he began his mission work, the vast extent of his labors (all of Ireland) and how the seeds he planted continued to grow and flourish, one can only admire the kind of man Patrick must have been. The holiness of a man is known only by the fruits of his work.

QUOTE: From the "Breastplate of St. Patrick": Christ shield me this day: Christ with me, Christ before me, Christ behind me, Christ in me, Christ beneath me, Christ above me, Christ on my right, Christ on my left, Christ when I lie down, Christ when I arise, Christ in the heart of every person who thinks of me, Christ in the mouth of every person who speaks of me, Christ in the eye that sees me, Christ in the ear that hears me.

March 18   *Optional*

CYRIL OF JERUSALEM,
bishop and doctor
(315?-386)

Problems in the Church today are minor compared with the reverberations of the Arian heresy that denied the divinity of Christ. Cyril was to be caught up in the controversy, accused (later) of Arianism by St. Jerome, and ultimately vindicated both by the men of his own time and by being declared a Doctor of the Church in 1822.

Raised in Jerusalem, well educated, especially in the Scriptures, he was ordained priest by the bishop of Jerusalem and given the task of catechizing those preparing for baptism (during Lent) and those newly baptized (during the week after Easter). These *Catechesis* remain valuable as examples of the ritual and theology of the Church in mid-fourth century.

There are conflicting reports about the circumstances of his becoming bishop of Jerusalem. It is certain that he was validly consecrated by bishops of the province. Since one of them was an Arian, Acacius, it may have been expected that his "cooperation" would follow. Conflict soon rose between Cyril and Acacius, bishop of the rival nearby see of Caeserea. Cyril was summoned to a council, accused of insubordination and of selling Church property to relieve the poor. Probably, however, a theological difference was also involved. He was condemned, driven from Jerusalem, and later vindicated, not without some association and help of Semi-Arians. Half his episcopate was spent in exile (his first experience was repeated twice). He finally returned to find Jerusalem torn with heresy, schism and strife, racked with crime. Even St. Gregory of Nyssa, sent to help, left in despair.

They both went to the (second ecumenical) Council of Constantinople, where the amended form of the Nicene Creed was promulgated. Cyril accepted the word "consubstantial" (i.e., of Christ and the Father). Some said it was an act of repentance; but the bishops of the Council praised him as a champion of orthodoxy against the Arians. Though not friendly with the greatest defender of orthodoxy against the Arians, Cyril may be counted among those whom Athanasius called "brothers, who mean what we mean, and differ only about the word ('consubstantial')."

COMMENT: Those who fancy that the lives of saints are simple and placid, untouched by the vulgar breath of controversy, are rudely shocked by history. Yet is should be no surprise that saints, indeed all Christians, will experience the same difficulties as their Master. The definition of truth is an endless, complex pursuit, and good men and women have suffered the pain of both controversy and error. Intellectual, emotional and political roadblocks may slow up men like Cyril for a time. But their lives taken as a whole are monuments to honesty and courage.

QUOTE: It is not only among us, who are marked with the name of Christ, that the dignity of faith is great; all the business of the world, even of those outside the Church, is accomplished by faith. By faith, marriage laws join in union persons who were strangers to one another. By faith, agriculture is sustained; for a man does not endure the toil involved unless he believes he will reap a harvest. By faith, seafaring men, entrusting themselves to a tiny wooden craft, exchange the solid element of the land for the unstable motion of the waves. Not only among us does this hold true but also, as I have said, among those outside the fold. For though they do not accept the Scriptures but advance certain doctrines of their own, yet even these they receive on faith (*Catechesis* V).

March 19   *Solemnity*

JOSEPH, HUSBAND OF MARY

The Bible pays Joseph the highest compliment: he was a "just" man. The quality meant a lot more than faithfulness in paying debts.

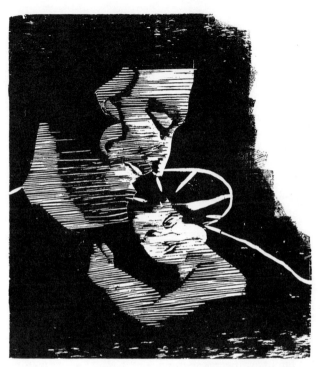

When the Bible speaks of God "justifying" a man, it means that God, the all-holy or "righteous" One, so transforms a man that he shares somehow in God's own holiness, and hence it is really "right" for God to love him. In other words, God is not playing games, acting as if we were lovable when we are not.

By saying Joseph was "just," the bible means that he was one who was completely open to all that God wanted to do for him. He became holy by opening himself totally to God.

The rest we can easily surmise. Think of the kind of love with which he wooed and won Mary, and the depth of the love they shared during their marriage.

It is no contradiction to Joseph's manly holiness that he decided to divorce Mary when she was found to be with child. The important words of the bible are that he planned to do this "quietly" because he was "a just man unwilling to expose her to the law."

The just man was simply, joyfully, wholeheartedly obedient to God — in marrying Mary, in naming Jesus, in shepherding the precious pair to Egypt, in bringing them to Nazareth, in the undetermined number of years of quiet faith and courage.

COMMENT: The Bible tells us nothing of Joseph in the years after the return to Nazareth except the incident of finding Jesus in the temple. Perhaps this can be taken to mean that God wants us to realize that the holiest family was like every other family, that the circumstances of life for the holiest family were like those of every family, so that when Jesus' mysterious nature began to appear, people couldn't believe that he came from such humble beginnings: "Isn't this the carpenter's son? Isn't Mary known to be his mother?" It was almost as indignant as "Can any good come from Nazareth?"

QUOTE: "When hunger came to be felt throughout the land of Egypt and the people cried to Pharaoh for bread, Pharaoh directed all the Egyptians to go to Joseph and do whatever he told them. When the famine spread throughout the land, Joseph opened all the cities that had grain and rationed it to the Egyptians. In fact, all the world came to Joseph to obtain rations of grain, for famine had gripped the whole world" (Genesis 41: 55-57).

TURIBIUS OF MONGROVEJO, bishop
(1538-1606)

Together with Rose of Lima, Turibius is the first known saint of the New World, serving the Lord in Peru, South America for 26 years.

Born in Spain and educated for the law, he became so brilliant a scholar that he was made professor of law at the University of Salamanca and eventually became chief judge of the Inquisition at Granada. He succeeded too well. But he was not sharp enough a lawyer to prevent a surprising sequence of events.

When the archbishopric of Lima in Spain's Peruvian colony became vacant, it was decided that Turibius was the man needed to fill the post: he was the one person with the strength of character and holiness of spirit to heal the scandals that had infected that area.

He cited all the canons that forbade giving laymen ecclesiastical dignities, but he was overruled. He was ordained priest and bishop and sent to Peru where he found colonialism at its worst. The Spanish conquerors were guilty of every sort of oppression of the native population. Abuses among the clergy were flagrant, and he devoted his energies (and suffering) to this area first.

He began the long and arduous visitation of an immense archdiocese, studying the language, staying two or three days in each place often with neither bed nor food. He confessed every morning to his chaplain, and celebrated Mass with intense fervor.

71

Among those to whom he gave the sacrament of confirmation was St. Rose of Lima, and possibly St. Martin de Porres. After 1590 he had the help of another great missionary, Francis Solanus.

His people, though very poor, were sensitive, dreading to accept public charity from others. Turibius solved the problem by helping them anonymously.

COMMENT: The Lord indeed writes straight with crooked lines. Against his will, and from the unlikely springboard of an Inquisition tribunal, this man became the Christlike shepherd of a poor and oppressed people. God gave him the gift of loving others as they needed it.

STORY: When Turibius undertook the reform of the clergy, as well as unjust officials, he naturally suffered opposition. Some tried, in human fashion, to "explain" God's law in such a way as to sanction their accustomed way of life. He answered them in the words of Tertullian, "Christ said, 'I am the truth'; he did not say, 'I am the custom.'"

April 2   *Optional*

FRANCIS OF PAOLA, hermit
(1416-1507)

Francis of Paola was a man who deeply loved contemplative solitude and wished only to be the "least in the household of God." Yet, when the Church called him to actively serve in the world, he became a miracle worker and influenced the course of nations.

After accompanying his parents on a pilgrimage to Rome and Assisi, he began to live as a contemplative hermit in a remote cave on the seacoast near Paola. Before he was 20, he received his first followers who had come to imitate his way of life. Seventeen years later, when his disciples had grown in number, Francis established a rule for his austere community and sought church approval. This was the founding of the Hermits of St. Francis of Assisi, who were approved by the Holy See in 1474.

In 1492, Francis changed the name of his community to "Minims" because he wanted them to be known as the least (minimi) in the household of God. Humility was to be the hallmark of the brothers as it had been in Francis' personal life. Besides the vows of poverty, chastity and obedience, Francis enjoined his followers the fourth obligation of a perpetual Lenten fast. He felt that heroic mortification was necessary as a means for spiritual growth.

It was Francis' desire to be a contemplative hermit, yet he believed that God was calling him to the apostolic life. He began to use the gifts he had received, such as the gifts of miracles and prophesy, to minister to the people of God. A defender of the poor and oppressed, Francis incurred the wrath of King Ferdinand of Naples for the admonitions he directed towards the king and his sons.

Following the request of Pope Sixtus IV, Francis traveled to Paris to help Louis XI of France prepare for his death (see story). While ministering to the king, Francis was able to influence the course of national politics. He helped to restore peace between

France and Britanny by advising a marriage between the ruling families, and between France and Spain by persuading Louis XI to return some disputed land.

Francis died while at the French court.

COMMENT: The life of Francis of Paola speaks plainly to an over-active world. He was a contemplative man called to active ministry and must have felt keenly the tension between prayer and service. Yet in Francis' life it was a productive tension for he clearly utilized the fruits of contemplation in his ministry which came to involve the workings of nations. He responded so readily and so well to the call of the Church from a solid foundation in prayer and mortification. When he went out to the world, it was not he who worked but Christ working through him — "the least in the household of God."

STORY: The King of France, Louis XI, was slowly dying after an apoplectic seizure. He sent to Italy to beg Francis to come and heal him, making many promises to assist him and his order. Francis refused, until the king appealed to the pope, who ordered him to go. Louis fell on his knees and begged Francis to heal him. The saint replied that the lives of kings are in the hands of God and have their appointed limits: prayer should be addressed to him.

Many meetings followed. Though Francis was an unlearned man, those who heard him have testified that his words were so full of wisdom that all present were convinced that the Holy Spirit was speaking through him. By prayer and example he brought about a change of heart in the king, who died peacefully in his arms.

ISIDORE OF SEVILLE,
bishop and doctor
(560?-636)

The 76 years of Isidore's life were a time of conflict and growth for the Church in Spain. The Visigoths had invaded the land a century and a half earlier and shortly before Isidore's birth they set up their own capital. They were Arians — Christians who said Christ was not God. Thus Spain was split in two: one people (Catholic Romans) struggled with another (Arian Goths).

Isidore reunited Spain, making it a center of culture and learning, a teacher and guide for other European countries whose culture was also threatened by barbarian invaders.

Born in Carthagena of a family that included three other saints, he was educated (severely) by his elder brother, whom he succeeded as bishop of Seville.

An amazingly learned man, he was sometimes called "The School-master of the Middle Ages" because the encyclopedia he wrote was used as a textbook for nine centuries. He required seminaries to be built in every diocese, wrote a rule for religious orders and founded schools that taught every branch of learning. Isidore wrote numerous books, including a dictionary, an encyclopedia, a history of the Goths and a history of the world beginning with creation! He completed the Mozarabic liturgy which is still in use in Toledo, Spain.

He continued his austerities even as he approached 80. During the last six months of his life, he increased his charities so much that his house was crowded from morning till night with the poor of the countryside.

COMMENT: Our troubled country can well use Isidore's spirit of combining learning and holiness. Loving, understanding knowledge can heal and bring a broken people back together. We are not barbarians like the invaders of Isidore's Spain. But people who are swamped by riches and over-whelmed by scientific and technological advances can lose much of their understanding love for one another.

STORY: Once, when Isidore was a boy, he ran away from home and from school. His brother Leander, some 20 years older than he, was his teacher, and a very demanding one. While Isidore sat by himself out in the woods, loafing, he watched some drops of water falling on a rock. Then he noticed — the dripping water had worn a hole in the hard rock! The thought came to him that he could do what the little drops of water did. Little by little, by sticking to it, he could learn all his brother demanded, and maybe even more.

April 5   *Optional*

VINCENT FERRER, priest
(1350?-1419)

The polarization in the Church today is a mild breeze compared with the tornado that ripped the church apart during the lifetime of this saint. If any saint is a patron of reconciliation, Vincent Ferrer is.

Despite parental opposition, he entered the Dominican Order in his native Spain at 19. After brilliant studies, he was ordained priest by Cardinal Peter de Luna — who would figure tragically in his life.

Of a very ardent nature, he practiced the austerities of the Order with great energy. He was chosen prior of the Dominican monastery in Valencia shortly after his ordination.

The Western Schism divided Christianity first between two, then three, popes. Clement lived at Avignon in France, Urban in Rome. Vincent was convinced the election of Urban was invalid (though Catherine of Siena was just as devoted a supporter of the Roman pope). In the service of Cardinal de Luna, he worked to persuade Spaniards to follow Clement. When Clement died, Cardinal de Luna was elected at Avignon and became Benedict XIII.

Vincent worked for him as apostolic penitentiary and Master of the Sacred Palace. But the new pope did not resign as all candidates in the conclave had sworn to do. He remained stubborn despite being deserted by the French king and nearly all of the cardinals.

Vincent became disillusioned and very ill, but finally took up the work of simply "going through the world preaching Christ," though he felt that any renewal in the Church depended on healing the schism. An eloquent and fiery preacher, he spent the last 20 years of his life spreading the Good News in Spain, France, Switzerland, the Low Countries and Lombardy, stressing the need of repentance and the fear of coming judgment (he became known as the "Angel of the Judgment").

He tried, unsuccessfully, in 1408 and 1415, to persuade his former friend to resign. He finally concluded that Benedict was not the true pope. Though very ill, he mounted the pulpit before an assembly over which Benedict himself was presiding and thundered his denunciation of the man who had ordained him priest. Benedict fled for his life, abandoned by those who had formerly supported him. Strangely, Vincent had no part in the Council of Constance which settled the schism.

COMMENT: The split in the Church at the time of Vincent Ferrer should have been fatal — 36 long years of having two "heads." We cannot imagine what condition the Church today would be in if, since the beginning of World War II, half the world had followed a succession of popes in Rome, and half, an equally "official" number of popes in, say, Rio de Janiero. It is an ongoing miracle that the Church has not long since been shipwrecked on the rocks of pride and ignorance, greed and ambition. Contrary to Lowell's words, "Truth forever on the scaffold, wrong forever on the throne," we believe that "truth is mighty, and it shall prevail" — but it sometimes takes a long time.

QUOTE: (From the litanies of St. Vincent)
  Precious stone of virginity
  Flaming torch of charity
  Mirror of penance
  Trumpet of eternal salvation
  Flower of heavenly wisdom
  Vanquisher of demons

JOHN BAPTIST DE LA SALLE, priest
(1651-1719)

Complete dedication to what he saw as God's will for him dominates the life of John Baptist de LaSalle. In 1950, Pope Pius XII named him patron of school teachers for his efforts in upgrading school instruction.

As a young 17th century Frenchman, John had everything going for him: scholarly bent, good looks, noble family background, money, refined upbringing. At the early age of 11, he received the tonsure and started preparation for the priesthood, to which he was ordained at 27. He seemed assured then of a life of dignified ease and a high position in the Church.

But God had other plans for John, which were gradually revealed to him in the next several years. During a chance meeting with M. Nyel of Raven, he became interested in the creation of schools for poor boys in Raven, where he was stationed. Though the work was extremely distasteful to him at first, he became more involved in working with the deprived youths.

Once convinced that this was his divinely appointed mission, John threw himself wholeheartedly into the work, left home and family, abandoned his position as canon at Rheims, gave away his fortune and reduced himself to the level of the poor to whom he devoted his entire life.

The remainder of his life was closely entwined with the community of religious men he founded, the

Brothers of the Christian School (Christian Brothers). This community grew rapidly and was successful in educating boys of poor families using methods designed by John, preparing teachers in the first training-college for teachers and also setting up homes and schools for young delinquents of wealthy families. The motivating element in all these endeavors was the desire to become a good Christian.

Yet even in his success, John did not escape experiencing many trials: heartrending disappointments and defections among his disciples, bitter opposition from the secular schoolmasters who resented his new and fruitful methods and persistent opposition from the Jansenists of his time, whose heretical doctrines John resisted vehemently all his life.

Afflicted with asthma and rheumatism in his last years, he died on Good Friday at 68 and was canonized in 1900.

COMMENT: Complete dedication to one's calling by God, whatever it may be, is a rare quality. Jesus asks us to "love the Lord your God with *all* your soul, with *all* your mind and with *all* your strength" (Mk. 12,30). Paul gives similar advice: "Whatever you do, work at it with your *whole being*" (Colossians 3, 23).

QUOTE: "What is nobler than to mould the character of the young? I consider that he who knows how to form the youthful mind is truly greater than all painters, sculptors and all others of that sort" (St. John Chrysostum; from *Breviary* for Feast of St. John Baptist de LaSalle).

STANISLAUS OF CRACOW,
bishop and martyr
(1030-1079)

Anyone who reads the history of Eastern Europe cannot help but chance on the name of Stanislaus, the saintly but tragic Bishop of Cracow, patron of Poland. He is remembered with Saints Thomas More and Thomas a' Becket for vigorous opposition to the evils of an unjust government.

Born in Szczepanow near Cracow on July 26, 1030, he was ordained priest after being educated in the cathedral schools of Gniezno, then capital of Poland, and at Paris. He was appointed preacher and archdeacon to the bishop of Cracow, where his eloquence and example brought about real conversion in many of his penitents, both clergy and laity. He became bishop of Cracow in 1072.

During an expedition against the Grand Duchy of Kiev, Stanislaus became involved in the political situation of Poland. Known for his outspokenness, he aimed his attacks at the evils of the peasantry and the king, especially the unjust wars and immoral acts of King Boleslaus II.

The king first excused himself, then made a show of penance, then relapsed into his old ways. Stanislaus continued his open opposition in spite of charges of treason and threats of death, finally excommunicating the king. The latter, enraged, ordered soldiers to kill the bishop. When they refused, the king killed him with his own hands.

Forced to flee to Hungary, Boleslaus supposedly

spent the rest of his life as a penitent in the Benedictine Abbey in Osiak, Hungary.

COMMENT: John the Baptist, Thomas a' Becket, Thomas More, Stanislaus are a few of the prophets who dared to denounce corruption in high places. They follow in the footsteps of Jesus himself, who pointed the finger at the moral corruption in the religious leadership of his day. It is a risky business: "Let him who is without sin cast the first stone."

QUOTE: "Men desire authority for its own sake that they may bear a rule, command and control other men, and live uncommanded and uncontrolled themselves" (St. Thomas More, *A Dialogue of Comfort*).

April 13   *Optional*

MARTIN I, pope and martyr
(d. 655)

When Martin I became pope in 649, Constantinople was the capital of the Byzantine empire and the Patriarch of Constantinople was the most influential church leader in the eastern Christian world. The struggles that existed within the Church at that time were magnified by the close cooperation of emperor and patriarch.

A teaching, strongly supported in the East, held that Christ had no human will. Twice emperors had officially favored this position, Heraclius by publishing a formula of faith and Constans II by silencing the issue of one or two wills in Christ.

Shortly after assuming the office of the papacy (which he did without first being confirmed by the emperor), Martin held a council at the Lateran in which the imperial documents were censured, and in which the Patriarch of Constantinople and two of his predecessors were condemned. Constans II, in response, tried first to turn bishops and people against the pope.

Failing in this and in an attempt to kill the pope, the emperor sent troops to Rome to seize Martin and to bring him back to Constantinople. Martin, already in poor health, offered no resistance, returned with the exarch Calliopas and was then submitted to various imprisonments, tortures and hardships. Although condemned to death, and with some of the torture imposed already carried out, Martin was saved from execution by the pleas of a repentant Paul, Patriarch of Constantinople, who himself was gravely ill.

Martin died shortly thereafter, his tortures and cruel treatment taking their toll. He is the last of the popes to be venerated as a martyr.

COMMENT: The real significance of "martyr" comes not from the dying but from the witnessing, which the word means in its derivation. A person who is willing to give up everything, his most precious possessions, his very life, puts a supreme value on the cause or belief for which he sacrifices. Martyrdom, dying for the faith, is an incidental extreme to which some have had to go to manifest their belief in Christ. A living faith, a life that exemplifies Christ's teaching throughout, and that in spite of difficulties, is required of all Christians. Martin I might have temporized, he might have sought means to ease his lot, to make some accommodations with the civil rulers.

QUOTE: The breviary of the Orthodox Church, viz., pays tribute to Martin: "Glorious definer of the Orthodox Faith ... sacred chief of divine dogmas, unstained by error ... true reprover of heresy ... foundation of bishops, pillar of the Orthodox Faith, teacher of religion ... Thou didst adorn the divine see of Peter, and since from this divine Rock, thou didst immovably defend the Church, so now thou art glorified with him."

April 21   *Optional*

ANSELM, bishop and doctor
(1033-1109)

Indifferent toward religion as a young man, Anselm became one of the Church's greatest theologians and leaders. He received the title "Father of Scholasticism" for his attempt to analyze and illumine the truths of faith through the aid of reason.

At 15, Anselm wanted to enter a monastery, but was refused acceptance because of his father's opposition. Twelve years later, after careless disinterest in religion and years of wordly living, he finally fulfilled his desire to be a monk. He entered the monastery of Bec in Normandy and three years later was elected prior, and 15 years later was unanimously chosen abbot.

Considered an original and independent thinker, Anselm was admired for his patience and gentleness and teaching skill. Under his leadership, the Abbey of Bec became a monastic school, influential in philosophical and theological studies.

During these years, at the community's request, Anselm began publishing his theological works comparable to those of St. Augustine. His best known work is the book *Cur Deus Homo (Why God Became Man)*.

At 60, against his will, Anselm was appointed Archbishop of Canterbury in 1093. Although his appointment was opposed at first by England's King William Rufus and later accepted, Rufus persistently refused to cooperate with efforts to reform the Church.

Anselm finally went into voluntary exile until Rufus died in 1100. He was then recalled to England by Rufus' brother and successor, Henry I. Disagreeing fearlessly with Henry over the king's right to invest England's bishops, Anselm spent another three years in exile in Rome.

His care and concern extended to the very poorest people and was the first in the Church to oppose the slave trade. Anselm obtained from the National Council at Westminster, the passage of a resolution prohibiting the sale of men.

COMMENT: Anselm, like every true follower of Christ, had to carry his cross, especially in the form of opposition and conflict with those in political control. Though personally a mild and gentle man and a lover of peace, he would not back off from conflict and persecution when principles were at stake.

QUOTE: "No one will have any other desire in heaven than what God wills; and the desire of one will be the desire of all; and the desire of all and of each one will also be the desire of God" (St. Anselm, *Opera Omnis,* Letter 112).

April 23   *Optional*

GEORGE, martyr

If Mary Magdalen was the victim of misunderstanding, George is the object of a vast amount of imagination. There is every reason to believe that he was a real martyr who suffered at Lydda in Palestine, probably before the time of Constantine. The Church adheres to his memory, but not to the legends surrounding his life.

That he was willing to pay the supreme price to follow Christ is what the Church believes. And it is enough.

The story of George's slaying the dragon, rescuing the king's daughter and converting Libya is a 12th century Italian fable.

George was a favorite patron saint of crusaders, as well as of Eastern soldiers in earlier times. He is a patron saint of England, Portugal, Germany, Aragon, Genoa and Venice.

COMMENT: Human nature seems unable to be satisfied with mere cold historical data. Americans have Washington and Lincoln, but we somehow need Paul Bunyan, too. The life of St. Francis of Assisi is inspiring enough, but for centuries the Italians have found his spirit in the *Fioretti,* too. Santa Claus is the popular extension of the spirit of St. Nicholas. Both fact and legend are human ways of illumining the mysterious truth about the One who alone is holy.

QUOTE: "When we look at the lives of those who have faithfully followed Christ, we are inspired with a new reason for seeking the city which is to come" (Vatican II, Constitution on the Church, 50).

April 24   *Optional*

FIDELIS OF SIGMARINGEN, priest and martyr
(1577-1622)

If a poor man needed some clothing, Fidelis would often give the man the clothes right off his back. Complete generosity to others characterized this saint's life.

Born in 1577, Mark Rey (Fidelis was his religious name) became a lawyer who constantly upheld the causes of the poor and oppressed people. Nicknamed "The Poor Man's Lawyer," Fidelis soon grew disgusted with the corruption and injustice he saw among his colleagues. He dropped his law career to become a priest, joining his brother George as a Franciscan friar of the Capuchin order. His wealth was divided between needy seminarians and the poor.

As a follower of Francis, Fidelis continued his devotion to the weak and needy. Once during a severe epidemic in a city where he was guardian of a friary, Fidelis cared for and cured many sick soldiers.

He was appointed head of a group of Capuchins sent to preach against the Calvinists and Zwinglians in Switzerland. Almost certain violence threatened. Those who observed the mission felt that success was more attributable to the prayer in which Fidelis spent his nights than to his sermons and instructions.

He was accused of being an opponent of the peasants' national aspirations for independence from Austria. While he was preaching at Seewis, to which he had gone against the advice of his friends, a gun was fired at him, but he escaped unharmed. A Protestant offered to shelter Fidelis, but he declined, saying his life was in God's hands. On the road back, he was set upon by a group of armed men and killed.

COMMENT: Fidelis' constant prayer was that he be kept completely faithful to God and not give in to any lukewarmness or apathy. He was often heard to exclaim, "Woe to me if I should prove myself but a half-hearted soldier in the service of my thorn-crowned Captain." His prayer against apathy, and his concern for the poor and weak make him a saint whose example is valuable today. The modern Church is calling us to follow the example of "The Poor Man's Lawyer" by sharing ourselves and our talents with those less fortunate and by working for justice in the world.

QUOTE: "Action on behalf of justice and participation in the transformation of the world fully appear to us as a constitutive dimension of the preaching of the Gospel, or, in other words, of the Church's mission for the redemption of the human race and its liberation from every oppressive situation" ("Justice in the World," Synod of Bishops, 1971).

April 25   *Feast*

MARK, evangelist

Most of what we know about Mark comes directly from the New Testament. He is usually identified with the Mark of Acts 12, 12 (when Peter escaped from prison, he went to the home of Mark's mother).

Paul and Barnabas took him along on the first missionary journey, but for some reason Mark returned alone to Jerusalem. It is evident, from Paul's refusal to let Mark accompany him on the second journey, despite Barnabas' insistence, that Mark had displeased Paul. Later, Paul asks Mark to visit him in prison, so we may assume the trouble did not last long.

The oldest and the shortest of the four Gospels, Mark emphasizes Jesus' rejection by men while being God's triumphant envoy. Probably written for Gentile converts in Rome — after the death of Peter and Paul, sometime between 60 and 70 A.D. — Mark's Gospel is the gradual manifestation of a "scandal": a crucified Messiah.

Evidently a friend of Mark (Peter called him "my son"), Peter is only one of the Gospel sources,

others being the Church in Jerusalem (Jewish roots) and the Church at Antioch (largely Gentile).

Like one other Gospel writer, Luke, Mark was not one of the Twelve Apostles. We cannot be certain whether he knew Jesus personally. Some scholars feel that the evangelist is speaking of himself when describing the arrest of Jesus in Gethsemani: "There was a young man following him who was covered by nothing but a linen cloth. As they seized him, he left the cloth behind and ran off naked."

Others hold Mark to be the first bishop of Alexandria, Egypt. Venice, famous for the Piazza San

Marco, claims Mark as its patron saint; the large basilica there is believed to contain his remains.

A winged lion is Mark's symbol. The lion derives from Mark's description of John the Baptist as a "voice crying in the desert" (Mk. 1,3), which artists compared to a roaring lion. The wings come from the application of Ezechiel's vision of four winged creatures to the evangelists.

COMMENT: Mark fulfilled in his life what every Christian is called to do: proclaim to all men the Good News which is the source of salvation. In particular, Mark's way was by writing. Others may proclaim the good news by music, drama, poetry or by teaching children around a family table.

QUOTE: There is very little in Mark which is not in the other Gospels. One of the four passages is: "Jesus also said: "This is how it is with the reign of God. A man scatters seed on the ground. He goes to bed and gets up day after day. Through it all the seed sprouts and grows without his knowing how it happens. The soil produces of itself first the blade, then the ear, finally the ripe wheat in the ear. When the crop is ready he 'wields the sickle, for the time is ripe for harvest.' "

April 28   *Optional*

PETER CHANEL, priest and martyr
(1803-1841)

Anyone who has worked in loneliness, with great adaptation required, and with little apparent success, will find a kindred spirit in Peter Chanel.

As a young priest he revived a parish in a "bad" district by the simple method of showing great devotion to the sick. Wanting to be a missionary, he joined the Society of Mary (Marists) at 28. Obediently, he taught in the seminary for five years. Then, as superior of seven Marists, he traveled to Western Oceania where he was entrusted with a vicariate. The bishop accompanying the missionaries left Peter and a brother on Futuna Island in the New Hebrides, promising to return in six months. The interval lasted five years.

Meanwhile he struggled with the unknown language and mastered it, making the difficult adjustment to life with whalers, traders and warring natives. Despite little apparent success and severe want, he maintained a serene and gentle spirit, endless patience and courage. A few natives had been baptized, a few more were being instructed. When the chieftain's son asked to be baptized, persecution by the chieftain reached a climax. Father Chanel was surrounded in his hut, clubbed to death, his body cut to pieces.

Within two years after his death, the whole island became Catholic and has remained so. Peter Chanel is the first martyr of Oceania and its patron.

COMMENT: Suffering for Christ means suffering because we are like Christ. Very often the opposition we meet is the result of our own selfishness or imprudence. We are not martyrs when we are "persecuted" by those who merely treat us as we treat them. A Christian martyr is one who, like Christ, is simply a witness of God's love, and brings out of men's hearts the good or evil that is already there.

QUOTE: "No one is a martyr for a conclusion, no one is a martyr for an opinion; it is faith that makes martyrs" (Cardinal Newman, *Discourses to Mixed Congregations*).

April 29   *Memorial*

CATHERINE OF SIENA, virgin
(1347-1380)

The value Catherine makes central in her short life and which sounds clearly and consistently through her experience is complete surrender to Christ. What is most impressive about her is that she learns to view her surrender to her Lord as a goal to be reached through time.

She was the 23rd child of Jacopo and Lapa Benincasa, and grew up as an intelligent, cheerful and intensely religious person. Whereas long hair is a parental problem today, Catherine disappointed her mother by cutting off her hair, as a protest against being overly encouraged to improve her appearance in order to attract a husband. Her father ordered her to be left in peace, and she was given a room of her own for prayer and meditation.

She entered the Dominican Third Order at 18, and spent the next three years in seclusion, prayer and austerity. Gradually a group of followers gathered around her — men and women, priests and religious. An active public apostolate grew out of her contemplative life. Her letters, mostly for spiritual instruction and encouragement of her followers, began to take more and more note of public affairs. Opposition and slander resulted from her mixing fearlessly with the world and speaking with the candor and authority of one completely committed to Christ. She was cleared of all charges at the Dominican General Chapter of 1374.

Her public influence reached great heights because of her evident holiness, her membership in the Dominican Order, and the deep impression she made on the pope. She worked tirelessly for the crusade against the Turks, and for peace between Florence and the pope.

In 1378, the Great Schism broke, splitting the allegiance of Christendom between two, then three, popes and putting even saints on opposing sides (see St. Vincent Ferrer, April 5). Catherine spent the last two years of her life in Rome, in prayer and pleading on behalf of the cause of Urban VI and the unity of the Church. She offered herself as a victim for the Church in its agony. She died surrounded by her "children."

Catherine ranks high among the mystics and spiritual writers of the Church. Her spiritual testament is found in *The Dialogue.*

COMMENT: Though she lived her life in a faith experience and spirituality far different from that of our own time, Catherine of Siena stands as a companion with us on the Christian journey in her undivided effort to invite the Lord to take flesh in her own life. Events which might make us wince or chuckle or even yawn fill her biographies: a mystical experience at six, childhood bethrothal to Christ, stories of harsh asceticism, her frequent ecstatic visions. Still, Catherine lived in an age which did not know the rapid change of 20th century mobile America. The value of her life for us today lies in her recognition of holiness as a goal to be sought over the course of a lifetime.

QUOTE: Catherine's book *Dialogue* contains four treatises — her testament of faith to the spiritual world. She wrote, "No one should judge that he has greater perfection because he performs great penances and gives himself in excess to the staying of the body than he who does less, inasmuch as neither virtue nor merit consists therein; for otherwise he would be an evil case, who from some legitimate reason was unable to do actual penance. Merit consists in the virtue of love alone, flavored with the light of true discretion, without which the soul is worth nothing."

April 30   *Optional*

PIUS V, pope
(1504-1572)

This is the pope whose job was to implement the historic Council of Trent. If we think Pope Paul has his difficulties today in implementing the Vatican Council II, Pius V had even greater problems after that historic council four centuries ago.

During his papacy, 1566-1572, Pius V was faced with the almost overwhelming responsibility of getting a shattered and scattered Church back on its feet. The family of God had been shaken by corruption, by the Reformation, by the constant threat of Turkish invasion and by the bloody bickering of the young nation-states. In 1545 a previous pope convened the Council of Trent in an attempt to deal with all these pressing problems. For 18 years the Church Fathers discussed, condemned, affirmed and decided upon a course of action. The Council closed in 1563.

Pius V was elected in 1566 and was charged with the task of implementing the sweeping reforms called for by the Council. He ordered the founding of seminaries for the proper training of priests. He published a new missal, a new breviary, a new catechism and established the Confraternity of Christian Doctrine (CCD) classes for the young. Pius zealously enforced legislation against abuses in the Church. He patiently served the sick and the poor by building hospitals, providing food for the hungry and giving money customarily used for the papal banquets to poorer Roman convents.

In striving to reform both Church and state Pius encountered vehement opposition from England's Queen Elizabeth and the Roman Emperor Maximilian II. Problems in France and in the Netherlands also hindered Pius's hopes for a Europe united against the Turks. Only at the last minute was he able to organize a fleet which won a decisive victory in the Gulf of Lepanto, off Greece, on October 7, 1571.

Pius's ceaseless papal quest for a renewal of the Church was grounded in his personal life as a Dominican friar. He spent long hours with his God in prayer, fasted rigorously, deprived himself of many customary papal luxuries and faithfully observed the Dominican Rule and its spirit.

COMMENT: In their personal lives and in their actions as Popes, Pius V and Paul VI have led the family of God in the process of interiorizing and implementing the new birth called for by the Spirit in the Councils of Trent and Vatican II. With zeal and patience Pius and Paul have pursued the changes urged by the Council Fathers. Like Pius and Paul, we too are called to constant change of heart and life.

QUOTE: "In a few moments you are about to leave the Council assembly to go out to meet mankind and to bring the good news of the gospel of Christ and of the renovation of his Church at which we have been working together for four years. In this universal assembly, in this privileged point of time and space, there converge together the past, the present, and the future. The past: for here, gathered in this spot, we have the Church of Christ with her tradition, her history, her Councils, her doctors, her saints; the present: we are taking leave of one another to go out toward the world of today with its miseries, its sufferings, its sins, but also with its prodigious accomplishments, values, and virtues; and the future is here in the urgent appeal of the peoples of the world for more justice, in their will for peace, in their conscious or unconscious thirst for a higher life, that life precisely which the Church of Christ can give and wishes to give to them" (from "Closing Messages of the Council: Pope Paul to the Council Fathers").

JOSEPH THE WORKER

Apparently in response to the "May Day" celebrations for workers sponsored by Communists, Pius XII instituted the feast of St. Joseph the Worker in 1955. But the relationship between Joseph and the cause of workers has a longer history.

In a constantly necessary effort to keep Jesus from being removed from ordinary human life, the Church has from the beginning proudly emphasized that Jesus was a carpenter, obviously trained by Joseph in both the satisfactions and the drudgery of that vocation. Man is like God not only in thinking and loving, but also in creating. Whether he makes a table or a cathedral, man is called to bear fruit with his hands and mind, ultimately for the building up of the Body of Christ.

COMMENT: "Yahweh God took the man and settled him in the garden of Eden to cultivate and take care of it" (Gen 2:15). The Father created all and asked man to continue the work of creation. Man finds his dignity in his work; in raising a family; in participating in the life of the Father's creation. Joseph the Worker was able to help participate in the deepest mystery of creation. Pius XII emphasizes this when he said, "the spirit flows to you and to all men from the heart of the God-man, Savior of the world, but certainly, no worker was ever more completely and profoundly penetrated by it than the foster father of Jesus, who lived with Him in closest intimacy and community of family life and work.

Thus, if you wish to be close to Christ, we again to-day repeat, 'Go to Joseph,' (Gen. 41:44)."

QUOTE: In *Brothers of Men,* Rene' Voillaume of the Little Brothers of Jesus speaks about ordinary work and holiness: "Now this holiness (of Jesus) became a reality in the most ordinary circumstances of life, those of word, of the family and the social life of a village, and this is an emphatic affirmation of the fact that the most obscure and humdrum human activities are entirely compatible with the perfection of the Son of God . . . . In relation to this mystery, involves *the conviction that the evangelical holiness proper to a child of God is possible in the ordinary circumstances of a man who is poor and obliged to work for his living."*

May 2   *Memorial*

ATHANASIUS, bishop and doctor
(295?-373)

Athanasius led a tumultuous but dedicated life of service to the Church. He was the great champion of the faith against the widespread heresy of Arianism. The vigor of his writings earned him the title of doctor of the Church.

Born of a Christian family in Alexandria and given a classical education, Athanasius entered the priesthood, became secretary to Alexander, the Bishop of Alexandria, and eventually was elevated to bishop himself. His predecessor, Alexander, had been an outspoken critic of a new movement growing in the East — Arianism.

When Athanasius assumed his role as Bishop of Alexandria, he continued the fight against Arianism. At first it seemed that the battle would be easily won and that Arianism would be condemned. Such, however, did not prove to be the case. The Council of Tyre was called and for several reasons which are still unclear, the Emperor Constantine exiled Athanasius to Northern Gaul. This was to be the first in a series of travels and exiles reminiscent of the life of St. Paul.

Constantine died, and his succeeding son restored Athanasius as bishop. This only lasted a year, however, for he was deposed once again by a coalition of Arian bishops. Athanasius took his case to Rome, and Pope Julius I called a synod to review the case and other related matters.

Five times he was exiled for his defense of the doctrine of Christ's divinity. During one period of his life, he enjoyed 10 years of relative peace — reading, writing and promoting the Christian life along the lines of the monastic ideal to which he was greatly devoted.

His dogmatic and historical writings are almost all polemic, directed against every aspect of Arianism. Among his ascetical writings, his Life of St. Anthony achieved astonishing popularity and contributed greatly to the establishment of monastic life throughout the Western Christian world.

COMMENT: Athanasius suffered many trials while he was Bishop of Alexandria. He was given the grace to remain strong against what probably seemed at times to be insurmountable opposition. Athanasius lived his office as bishop completely. He defended the true faith for his flock, regardless of the cost to himself. In today's world we are experiencing this same call to remain true to our faith no matter what opposition may be put in our path.

QUOTE: The hardships Athanasius suffered in exile, hiding, fleeing from place to place remind us of what Paul said of his own life: "I traveled continually, endangered by floods, robbers, my own people, the Gentiles; imperiled in the city, in the desert, at sea, by false brothers; in hunger and thirst and frequent fastings, in cold and nakedness. Leaving other sufferings unmentioned, there is that daily tension pressing on me, my anxiety for all the churches" (2 Cor. 11,26).

May 3   *Feast*

PHILIP and JAMES, apostles

JAMES, son of Alphaeus

We know nothing of this man but his name, and of course the fact that Jesus chose him to be one of the 12 pillars of the New Israel, his Church. He is not the James of Acts, son of Clopas, "brother" of Jesus and later bishop of Jerusalem, and the traditional author of the Epistle of James

PHILIP

Philip came from the same town as Peter and Andrew, Bethsaida in Galilee. Jesus called him directly, whereupon he sought out Nathanael and told him of the "one Moses spoke of."

Like the other apostles, Philip took a long time coming to realize who Jesus was. On one occasion, when Jesus saw the great multitude following him and wanted to give them food, he asked Philip where they should buy bread for the people to eat. St. John comments, "Jesus knew well what he intended to do, but he asked this to test Philip's response." Philip said "not even 200 days' wages could buy enough loaves to give each one of them a mouthful."

John's story is not a put-down of Philip. It was simply necessary for these men who were to be the foundation stones of the Church to see the clear distinction between man's total helplessness apart from God and his ability to be a bearer of the full force of divine power by God's gift.

On another occasion, we can almost hear the exasperation in Jesus' voice. After Thomas had complained that they did not know where Jesus was going, Jesus said "I *am* the way." If you really knew me, you would know my Father also. You have seen him." Then Philip said, "Lord, show us the Father, and that will be enough for us." (Enough!) Jesus answered, "Philip, after I have been with you all this time, you still do not know me? Whoever has seen me has seen the Father."

Possibly because Philip bore a Greek name, or because he was thought to be close to Jesus, some Gentile proselytes came to him and asked him to introduce them to Jesus. Philip went to Andrew, and Andrew went to Jesus. The reply of Jesus in John's Gospel is indirect; Jesus says that now his "hour" has come, that in a short time he will give his life for Jew and Gentile alike.

COMMENT: As in the case of the other apostles, we see a very "human" man who became a foundation stone of the Church, and we are reminded again that holiness and its consequent apostolate is entirely the gift of God, not a matter of human achieving. All power is God's power, even the power of human freedom to accept his gifts. "You will be clothed with power from on high," Jesus told Philip and the others. Their first commission had been to expel unclean spirits, heal diseases, announce the kingdom. They learned, gradually, that these externals were sacraments of an even greater miracle inside their persons — the divine power to love like God.

QUOTE: "He sent them . . . as sharers of his power, that they might make all peoples his disciples, sanctifying and governing them . . . They were fully confirmed in this mission on the day of pentecost, in accordance with the Lord's promise: 'You will receive power when the Holy Spirit comes upon you, and you shall be witnesses for me . . . even to the ends of the earth.' By everywhere preaching the gospel, which was accepted by their hearers under the influence of the Holy Spirit, the apostles gathered together the universal church, which the Lord established on the apostles and built upon blessed Peter, their chief, Christ Jesus remaining the supreme cornerstone" (Vatican II, Constitution on the Church, 19).

NEREUS and ACHILLEUS, martyrs
(1st cent.?)

Devotion to these two saints goes back to the fourth century, though almost nothing is known of their lives. They were pretorian soldiers of the Roman army, became Christians and were removed to the island of Terracina, where they were martyred. Their bodies were buried in a family vault, later known as the cemetery of Domitilla. Excavations by De Rossi in 1896 resulted in the discovery of their empty tomb in the undergound church built by Pope Siricius in 390.

Two hundred years after their death Pope Gregory the Great delivered his 28th homily on the occasion of their feast. "These saints, before whom we are assembled, despised the world and trampled it under their feet when peace, riches and health gave it charms."

COMMENT: As in the case of many early martyrs, the Church clings to her memories though the events are clouded in the mists of history. It is a heartening thing for all Christians to know that they have a noble heritage. Our brothers and sisters in Christ have stood in the same world in which we live — militarist, materialist, cruel and cynical — yet transfigured from within by the presence of the Living One. Our own courage is enlivened by the heroes and heroines who have gone before us marked by the sign of faith and the wounds of Christ.

QUOTE: Pope Damasus wrote an epitaph for them

in the fourth century. The text is known from travellers who read it while the slab was still entire, but the broken fragments found by De Rossi are sufficient to identify it: "The martyrs Nereus and Achilleus had enrolled themselves in the army and exercised the cruel office of carrying out the orders of the tyrant, being ever ready, through the constraint of fear, to obey his will. O miracle of faith! Suddenly they cease from their fury, they become converted, they fly from the camp of their wicked leader; they throw away their shields, their armor and their blood-stained javelins. Confessing the faith of Christ, they rejoice to bear testimony to its triumph. Learn now from the words of Damasus what great things the glory of Christ can accomplish."

May 12   *Optional*

PANCRAS, martyr
(d. 304?)

St. Pancras Railway Station in London got its name from an early Christian martyr about whom we have very little information. He is said to have been martyred at 14 during the persecution of Diocletian. He was buried in a cemetery which later was named after him. Gregory the Great built a monastery for Benedictines and when Augustine of Canterbury (a Benedictine) came to England he named the first church he erected after Pancras. Hence the name of the railway station.

Pancras (Pancratius) appears in fictionalized

form in Cardinal Wiseman's novel *Fabiola*. German farmers had a saying that three saints whose names are similar: Pancras, Servatz and Bonifatz were the "ice men" because it was unseasonably chilly on their feast days: May 12, 13, 14.

COMMENT: Again we have a saint about whom almost nothing is known, but whose life and death are cherished in the church's memory. Details fall away, or are mixed with the fantasy of legend. But a single, powerful fact remains: he died for Christ, and his heroism sent a wave of inspiration through the Church of his day. It is good for us to share that feeling.

QUOTE: "They will manhandle and persecute you, summoning you to synagogues and prisons, bringing you to trial before kings and governors, all because of my name. I beg you resolve not to worry about your defense beforehand, for I will give you words and a wisdom which none of your adversaries can take exception to or contradict" (Lk. 21:12-15).

May 14   *Feast*

MATTHIAS, apostle

"At one point during those days" after the Ascension, Peter stood up in the midst of the brothers. At least 120 were gathered. Now that Judas had betrayed his ministry, it was necessary to fulfill the Scripture which said, "Let another take his office."

"It is fitting, therefore," Peter said, "that one of those who was in our company while the Lord Jesus moved among us, from the baptism of John until the day he was taken up from us, should be named witness with us to his resurrection."

They nominated two men: Joseph Barsabbas and Matthias. They prayed, and drew lots. The choice fell upon Matthias, who was added to the Eleven.

Matthias is not mentioned by name anywhere else in the New Testament.

COMMENT: What was the holiness of Matthias? Obviously he was suited for apostleship by the experience of being with Jesus from his baptism to his ascension. He must also have been suited personally, or he would not have been nominated for so great a responsibility. Must we not remind ourselves that the fundamental holiness of Matthias was his receiving gladly the relationship with the Father offered him by Jesus and completed by the Holy Spirit? If the apostles are the foundations of our faith by their witness, they must also be reminders, if only implicitly, that holiness is entirely a matter of God's giving, and it is offered to all, in the everyday circumstances of life. Man receives, and even for this God supplies the power of freedom.

QUOTE: Jesus speaks of the apostles' function of being judges, i.e., rulers. He said, "I give you my solemn word, in the new age when the Son of Man takes his seat upon a throne befitting his glory, you who have followed me shall likewise take your places on 12 thrones to judge the 12 tribes of Israel" (Mt 19, 28).

ISIDORE THE FARMER
(1070-1130)

Isidore has become the patron of farmers and rural communities. In particular he is the patron of Madrid, Spain, and of the U.S. National Rural Life Conference.

When he was barely old enough to wield a hoe, Isidore entered the service of John de Vergas, a wealthy landowner from Madrid, and worked faithfully on his estate outside the city for the rest of his life. He married a young woman as simple and upright as himself who also became a saint — Maria de la Cabeza. They had one son, who died as a child.

Isidore had deep religious instincts. He rose early in the morning to go to Church and spent many a holiday devoutly visiting the churches of Madrid and surrounding areas. All day long, as he walked behind the plough, he communed with God. His devotion, one might say, became a problem, for his fellow workers sometimes complained that he often showed up late because of lingering in Church too long.

He was known for his love of the poor, and there are accounts of Isidore's supplying them miraculously with food. He had a great concern for the proper treatment of animals.

He died May 15, 1130, and was declared a saint in 1622 with Ignatius, Francis Xavier, Teresa and Philip Neri. Together, the group is known in Spain as "The Five Saints."

COMMENT: Many implications can be found in a simple laborer achieving sainthood: physical labor has dignity; sainthood does not stem from status; contemplation does not depend on learning; the simple life is conducive to holiness and happiness. Legends about his angel helpers and the mysterious oxen indicate that his work was *not* neglected and his duties did *not* go unfulfilled. Perhaps the truth which emerges is: If you have your spiritual self in order, your earthly commitments will fall into order also. "Seek first the Kingdom of heaven," said the carpenter from Nazareth, "and all these other things will be given you besides" (Matt. 6,33).

QUOTE: "God blessed them, saying, 'Be fertile and multiply; fill the earth and subdue it . . . See, I give you every seed-bearing plant all over the earth and every tree that has seed-bearing fruit on it to be your food, and to all the animals of the land, all the birds of the air, and all the living creatures that crawl on the ground, I give all the green plants for food'" (Gen. 1, 28).

May 18   *Optional*

JOHN I, pope and martyr
(d. 526)

The phrase "Good Pope John" still awakens warm memories in the hearts of Catholics, Protestants and Jews. It seems there could only be *one* Pope John. Yet there were obviously 22 of them before John the 23rd. Strangely enough, John the First is the only one (so far) honored as a saint.

Pope John I inherited the Arian heresy, which denied the divinity of Christ. Italy had been ruled for 30 years by an emperor who espoused the heresy, though he treated the Catholics of the empire with toleration. His policy changed at about the time the young John was elected pope.

When the Eastern emperor began imposing severe measures on the Arians of his area, the Western emperor forced John to head a delegation to the East to soften the measures against the heretics. Little is known of the manner or outcome of the negotiations — designed to secure continued toleration of Catholics in the West.

When John returned to Rome, he found that the emperor had begun to suspect his friendship with his eastern rival.

On his way home, John was imprisoned when he reached Ravenna because the emperor suspected a conspiracy against his throne. Shortly after his imprisonment, John died, apparently from the treatment he had received.

COMMENT: We cannot choose the issues for which we have to suffer and perhaps die. John XXIII suffered the suspicion of the super-orthodox because he was friendly with all sorts of men. John I suffered because of a power-conscious emperor. Jesus suffered because of the suspicions of those who were threatened by his freedom, openness and powerlessness. "If you find that the world hates you, know it has hated me before you."

QUOTE: "By martyrdom a disciple is transformed into an image of his Master, who freely accepted death on behalf of the world's salvation; he perfects that image even to the shedding of blood. Though few are presented with such an opportunity, nevertheless all must be prepared to confess Christ before men, and to follow him along the way of the cross through the persecutions which the Church will never fail to suffer" (Vatican II, Constitution on the Church, 71).

BERNARDINE OF SIENA, priest
(1380-1444)

Most of the saints suffer great personal opposition, even persecution. Bernardine, by contrast, seems more like a human dynamo who simply took on the needs of the world.

He was the greatest preacher of his time journeying across Italy, calming strife-torn cities, attacking the paganism he found rampant, attracting crowds of 30,000, following St. Francis' admonition to preach about "vice and virtue, punishment and glory."

Compared with St. Paul by the pope, Bernardine had a keen intuition of the needs of the time, along with solid holiness, boundless energy and joy. He accomplished all this despite having a very weak and hoarse voice, miraculously improved later because of his devotion to Mary.

When he was 20, the plague was at its height in his hometown, Siena. Sometimes as many as 20 people died in one day at the hospital. Bernardine offered to run the entire establishment, and with the help of other young men, nursed patients there for four months. He escaped the plague but was so exhausted that a fever confined him for several months. He spent another year caring for a beloved aunt (his parents had died when he was a child) and at her death began to fast and pray to know God's will for him.

At 22, he entered the Franciscan Order and was ordained two years later. For almost a dozen years he lived in solitude and prayer, but his gifts ultimately caused him to be sent to preach. He always traveled on foot, sometimes speaking for hours in one place, then doing the same in another town.

Especially known for his devotion to the Holy Name of Jesus, Bernardine devised a symbol — IHS — the first three letters of the name of Jesus in Greek — in gothic letters on a blazing sun. This was to displace the superstitious symbols of the day, as well as the insignia of factions (e.g., Guelphs and Ghibellines). The devotion spread, and the symbol began to appear in churches, homes and public buildings. Opposition arose from those who thought it a dangerous innovation. Three attempts were made to have the pope take action against him, but Bernardine's holiness, orthodoxy and intelligence were evidence of his faithfulness.

General of a branch of the Franciscans, the Friars of the Strict Observance, he strongly emphasized scholarship and further study of theology and canon law. When he started there were 300 friars in the community; when he died there were 4,000. He returned to preaching the last two years of his life, dying "on the road."

COMMENT: Another dynamic saint once said, "I do not want what you have, I only want you. I will gladly spend myself and be spent for your sakes" (Paul to the Corinthians, II, 12:14). There is danger that we see only the whirlwind of activity in the Bernardines of faith — taking care of the sick, preaching, studying, administering, always driving — and forget the source of their energy. We should not say that Bernardine, like Francis, *could* have been a great contemplative if he had the chance. He had the chance, every day, and he took it.

STORY: At Bologna, Bernardine preached mightily against the evils of gambling. As was the custom, a huge bonfire was made in the public square, to be a holocaust consuming all the instruments of the vice — playing cards, dice and the like. A manufacturer of playing cards complained that Bernardine was taking away his livelihood. The saint told him to start making the symbol "IHS" and he made more money than ever before.

VENERABLE BEDE,
priest and doctor
(672?-735)

Bede is one of the few saints who was honored as such even during his lifetime. His writings were filled with such faith and learning that even while he was still alive, a Church Council ordered them to be read publicly in the churches.

At an early age Bede was entrusted to the care of the abbot of the monastery of St. Paul, Jarrow. The happy combination of genius under the instruction of scholarly, saintly monks produced in turn a saint and an extraordinary scholar, perhaps the most outstanding of his time. He was deeply versed in all the sciences of his times: natural philosophy, the philosophical principles of Aristotle, astronomy, arithmetic, grammar, ecclesiastical history, the lives of the saints, but especially Holy Scripture.

From the time of his ordination to the priesthood

at 30 (he had been ordained deacon at 19) till his death, he was ever occupied with learning, writing and teaching. Besides the many books that he copied, he composed 45 of his own, of which 30 were devoted to commentary on the Bible.

Although eagerly sought by kings and other notables, even Pope Sergius, Bede managed to remain in his own monastery till his death. Only once did he leave for a few months in order to teach in the school of the Archbishop of York.

Bede died in 735 praying his favorite prayer: "Glory be to the Father, and to the Son, and to the Holy Spirit. As in the beginning, so now, and forever."

His *Ecclesiastical History* is commonly regarded as of decisive importance in the art and science of writing history. A golden age was coming to an end at the time of Bede's death: it had fulfilled its purpose of preparing Western Christianity to assimilate the non-Roman barbarian North. Bede recognized the opening to a new day in the life of the Church even as it was happening.

COMMENT: Though his *History* is the greatest legacy Bede has left us, his work in all the sciences, and especially in Scripture, should not be overlooked. During his last Lent, he worked on a translation of the Gospel of St. John into English, completing it the day he died. But of this work "to break the word to the poor and unlearned" nothing remains today.

QUOTE: "We have not, it seems to me, amid all our discoveries, invented as yet anything better than the

Christian life which Bede lived, and the Christian death which he died" (C. Plummer, editor of *Ecclesiastical History*).

GREGORY VII, pope
(1020-1085)

The 10th century and the first half of the 11th were dark days for the Church partly because the papacy was the pawn of various Roman families. In 1049, things began to change when Pope Leo IX, a reformer, was elected. He brought a young monk named Hildebrand to Rome as his counsellor and special representative on important missions. He was to become Gregory VII.

Three evils plagued the Church then: simony (the buying and selling of sacred offices and things); the unlawful marriage of the clergy; and lay investiture (kings and nobles controlling the appointment of Church officials). To all of these Hildebrand directed his reformer's attention, first as counsellor to the popes and later (1073-85) as pope himself.

Gregory's papal letters stress the role of Bishop of Rome as the vicar of Christ and the visible center of unity in the Church. He is well known for his long dispute with Henry IV, the Holy Roman Emperor, over who should control the selection of bishops and abbots.

Gregory fiercely resisted any attack on the liberty of the Church. For this he suffered and finally died in exile. He said, "I have loved justice and hated iniquity; therefore I die in exile." Thirty years

116

later the Church finally won its struggle against lay investiture.

COMMENT: The Gregorian Reform, a milestone in the history of Christ's Church, was named after this man who tried to extricate the papacy and the whole Church from undue control by civil rulers. Against an unhealthy Church nationalism in some areas, Gregory reasserted the unity of the whole Church based on Christ, and expressed in the Bishop of Rome, the successor of St. Peter.

QUOTE: Gregory has much to say to our age in which civil or national religion is making subtle demands: "In every country, even the poorest of women is permitted to take a lawful husband according to the law of the land and by her own choice; but, through the desires and evil practices of the wicked, Holy Church, the bride of God and mother of us all, is not permitted lawfully to cling to her spouse on earth in accordance with divine law and her own will" (A Call to the Faithful).

May 25 *Optional*
MARY MAGDALENE DE' PAZZI,
virgin
(1566-1607)

Mystical ecstasy is the elevation of the spirit to God in such a way that the person is aware of this union with God and both internal and external senses are detached from the sensible world. Mary Magdalene de Pazzi was so generously given this special gift of God that she is called the Ecstatic Saint.

She was born into a noble family in Florence in 1566, when Florence was a great city and its first families had influence. The normal course would have been for Catherine Pazzi to have married nobly and enjoyed comfort. But she hardly followed the normal course. At nine she learned to meditate from the family confessor. She made her First Communion at the then early age of 10 and made a vow of virginity one month later. When 16, she entered the Carmelite convent in Florence because she could receive Communion daily there.

Catherine had taken the name Mary Magdalene and had been a novice for a year when she became critically ill. Death seemed near so her superiors let her make her profession of vows from a cot in the chapel in a private ceremony. Immediately after, she fell into an ecstasy that lasted about two hours. This was repeated after Communion on the following 40 mornings. These ecstasies were rich experiences of union with God and contained marvelous insights into divine truths.

As a safeguard against deception and to preserve the revelations, her confessor asked Mary Magdalene to dictate her experiences to sister secretaries. Over the next six years, five large volumes were filled. The first three books record ecstasies from May 27, 1584 through Pentecost week of 1585. This week was a preparation for a severe 5-year trial. The fourth book records that trial and the fifth is a collection of letters concerning reform and renewal. Another book, *Admonistions,* is a collection of her sayings arising from her experiences in the formation of religious.

The extraordinary was ordinary for this saint. She read the thoughts of others and predicted future events. During her lifetime, she appeared to several persons in distant places and cured a number of sick people.

It would be easy to dwell on the ecstasies and pretend that Mary Magdalene only had spiritual highs. This is far from true. It seems that God permitted her this special closeness to prepare her for the five years of desolation that followed when she experienced spiritual dryness. She was plunged into a state of darkness in which she saw nothing but what was horrible in herself and all around her. She had violent temptations and endured great physical suffering. She died in 1607 at 41 and was cannonized in 1669. Over 350 years later, her body is still uncorrupt.

COMMENT: God's gift of intimate union to mystics is a reminder to all of us of the eternal happiness of union he wishes to give us. The cause of mystical ecstasy in this life is the Holy Spirit, working through his gifts. The ecstasy occurs because of the weakness of the body and its powers to withstand the divine illumination, but as the body is purified and strengthened, ecstasy no longer occurs. On various aspects of ecstasy, see Teresa of Avila, *Interior Castle,* Sixth Mansions, Ch. 5, and John of the Cross, *Dark Night,* 2, 1-2.

QUOTE: There are many people today who see no purpose in suffering. Mary Magdalene de'Pazzi discovered saving grace in suffering. When she entered religious life she was filled with a desire to suffer during the rest of her life for Christ. The more she suffered, the greater grew her desire for it. Her dying words to her fellow sisters were: ". . . the last thing I ask of you — and I ask it in the name of our Lord Jesus Christ — is that you love him alone, that you trust implicitly in him and that you encourage one another continually to suffer for the love of him."

PHILIP NERI, priest
(1515-1595)

Philip Neri was a sign of contradiction, combining popularity with piety against the background of a currupt Rome and a disinterested clergy, the whole post-Renaissance malaise.

At an early age, he abandoned the chance to become a businessman, moved to Rome from Florence and devoted his life and individuality to God. After three years of philosophy and theology he gave up any thought of ordination. The next 13 years were spent in a vocation unusual at the time — that of a layman actively engaged in prayer and the apostolate.

As the Council of Trent was reforming the Church on a doctrinal level, Philip's appealing personality was winning him friends from all walks of society, from beggars to cardinals. He rapidly gathered around himself a group of laymen, won over by his audacious spirituality. Initially they met as an informal prayer and discussion group, and also served the needy of Rome.

At the urging of his confessor, he was ordained priest and soon became an outstanding confessor, gifted with the knack of piercing the pretenses and illusions of others, though always in a charitable manner and often with a joke. He arranged talks, discussions and prayers for his penitents in a room above the church. He sometimes led "excursions" to other churches, often with music and a picnic on the way.

Some of his followers became priests and lived together in community. This was the beginning of the Oratory, the religious institute he founded. A feature of their life was the daily afternoon service of four informal talks, with vernacular hymns and prayers. Palaestrina was one of Philip's followers, and composed music for the services.

The Oratory was finally approved after suffering through a period of being accused of being an assembly of heretics, where laymen preached and sang vernacular hymns! (Cardinal Newman founded the first English-speaking house of the Oratory.)

Philip's advice was sought by many of the prominent figures of his day. He is one of the influential figures of the Counter Reformation, mainly for converting to personal holiness many of the influential people within the Church itself. His characteristic virtues were humility and gaiety.

COMMENT: Many people wrongly feel that such an attractive and jocular personality as Philip's cannot be combined with an intense spirituality. Philip's life melts our rigid, narrow views of piety. His approach to sanctity was truly catholic, all-embracing and accompanied by a good laugh. Philip always wanted his followers to become not less, but more human through their striving for holiness.

QUOTE: Philip Neri prayed, "Let me get through today, and I shall not fear tomorrow."

May 27   *Optional*

AUGUSTINE OF CANTERBURY, bishop
(d. 605?)

In the year 596 a small party of some 30 monks set out from Rome to evangelize the Anglo-Saxons in England. Leading the group was Augustine, the prior of their monastery in Rome. Hardly had he and his men reached Gaul (France) when they heard stories of the ferocity of the Anglo-Saxons and of the treacherous waters of the English channel. Augustine returned to Rome and to the Pope who had sent them, St. Gregory the Great — only to be assured by him that their fears were groundless.

Augustine again set out and this time the group crossed the channel and landed in the territory of Kent ruled by King Ethelbert, a pagan married to a Christian. Ethelbert received them kindly, set up a residence for them in Canterbury and within the year, on Pentecost Sunday, 597, was himself baptized. After being consecrated a bishop in France, Augustine returned to Canterbury where he founded his see. He constructed a Church and monastery on the site where the present Cathedral, begun in 1070, now stands. As the Faith spread, additional sees were established at London and Rochester.

Work was sometimes slow and Augustine did not always meet with success. Attempts to reconcile the Anglo-Saxon Christians with the original Briton Christians (who had been driven into western England by Anglo-Saxon invaders) ended in dismal failure. Augustine failed to convince the Britons to give up certain Celtic customs at variance with Rome and to forget their bitterness, helping him evangelize their Anglo-Saxon conquerors.

Laboring patiently, Augustine wisely heeded the missionary principles — quite enlightened for the times — suggested by Pope Gregory the Great: purify rather than destroy pagan temples and customs; let pagan rites and festivals be taken over into Christian feasts; retain local customs as far as possible. The limited success Augustine achieved in England before his death in 604, a short seven years after he arrived in England, would eventually bear fruit long after in the conversion of England. Truly Augustine of Canterbury can be called the "Apostle of England."

COMMENT: Augustine of Canterbury comes across today as a very human saint, one who could suffer like many of us from a failure of nerve. For example, his first venture to England ended in a big U-turn back to Rome. He made mistakes and met failure in his peacemaking attempts with the Briton Christians. He often wrote to Rome for decisions on matters he could have decided on his own, had he been more self-assured. He even received mild warnings against pride from Pope Gregory who cautioned him to "fear lest, amidst the wonders that are done, the weak mind be puffed up by self-esteem." Augustine's perserverance amidst obstacles and only partial success teaches today's apostles and pioneers to struggle on despite frustrations and be satisfied with gradual advances.

QUOTE: In a letter to Augustine, Pope Gregory the Great wrote: "He who would climb to a lofty height must go by steps, not leaps."

June 1   *Memorial*

JUSTIN, martyr
(d. 165)

Justin never ended his quest for religious truth even when he converted to Christianity after years of studying various pagan philosophies.

As a young man, he was principally attracted to the school of Plato. However, he found that the Christian religion answered the great questions about life and existence better than the philosophers.

Upon his conversion he continued to wear the philosopher's mantle, and became the first Christian philosopher. He combined the Christian religion with the best elements in Greek philosophy. In his view, philosophy was a pedagogue of Christ, an educator that was to lead one to Christ.

Justin is known as an apologist, one who defended in writing the Christian religion against the attacks and misunderstandings of the pagans. Two of his apologies have come down to us; they are addressed to the Roman emperor and Senate.

For his staunch adherence to the Christian religion, Justin was beheaded in Rome in 165.

COMMENT: As patron of philosophers, Justin may inspire us to use our natural powers, especially our power to know and understand, in the service of Christ and to build up the Christian life within us. Since man is prone to error, especially in reference to the deep questions concerning life and existence, we should also be willing to correct and check our natural thinking in light of religious truth. Thus we will be able to say with the learned saints of the Church: I believe in order to understand, and I understand in order to believe.

QUOTE: "Philosophy is the knowledge of that which exists, and a clear understanding of the truth; and happiness is the reward of such knowledge and understanding" (Justin, *Dialogue with Trypho*, 3).

June 2   *Optional*
MARCELLINUS and PETER, martyrs
(d. 304)

Marcellinus and Peter were prominent enough in the memory of the church to be included among the saints of the Roman canon. Mention of their names is optional in our present Eucharistic Prayer I.

Marcellinus was a priest and Peter was an exorcist (strange that this order, one of the four "minor" orders has been dropped just at the time when Hollywood recognized the devil). They were beheaded during the persecution of Diocletian.

Pope Damasus wrote an epitaph apparently founded on the report of their executioner, and Constantine erected a basilica over the crypt in which they were buried in Rome. Numerous legends sprang from an early account of their death.

COMMENT: Why are these men included in our Eucharistic prayer, and given their own feast day, in spite of the fact that almost nothing is known about them? Probably because the Church respects its collective memory. They once sent an impulse of encouragement through the whole church. They made the ultimate step of faith.

QUOTE: "The Church has always believed that the apostles, and Christ's martyrs who had given the supreme witness of faith and charity by the shedding of their blood, are quite closely joined with us in Christ" (Vatican II, Constitution on the Church, 50).

June 3   *Memorial*

CHARLES LWANGA, martyr
(d. 1886)

One of 22 Ugandan martyrs, Charles Lwanga is the patron of youth and Catholic action in most of tropical Africa. He protected his fellow pages, ages 13-30, from the homosexual demands of the Bagandan ruler, Mwanga, and encouraged and instructed them in the Catholic faith during their imprisonment for refusing the demands.

For his own unwillingness to submit to the immoral acts and his efforts to safeguard the faith of his friends, Charles was burned to death at Namugongo, on June 3, 1886, by Mwanga's order.

Charles first learned of Christ's teachings from two retainers in the court of Chief Mawulugungu. While a catechumen, he entered the royal household as assistant to Joseph Mukaso, head of the court pages.

On the night of Mukaso's martyrdom for encouraging the African youths to resist Mwanga, Charles requested and received Baptism. Imprisoned with his friends, Charles' courage and belief in God inspired them to remain chaste and faithful.

The 22 martyrs were canonized by Pope Paul VI, on Oct. 18, 1964.

COMMENT: Like Charles Lwanga, we are all teachers and witnesses to Christian living by the examples of our own lives. We are all called upon to spread the Word of God, whether by word or deed. By remaining courageous and unshakable in our faith during times of great moral and physical temptation, we live as Christ lived.

QUOTE: On his African tour in 1969, Pope Paul VI told 22 young Ugandan converts that "being a Christian was a fine thing but not always an easy one."

BONIFACE, bishop and martyr
(672?-754)

Boniface, known as the Apostle of the Germans, was an English Benedictine monk who gave up the honors of an abbatial election to devote his life to the conversion of the Germanic tribes. Two characteristics stand out: his Christian orthodoxy and his fidelity to the Pope of Rome.

How absolutely necessary this orthodoxy and fidelity were, is borne out by the conditions he found on his first missionary journey in 719 at the request of Pope Gregory II. Paganism was a way of life. What Christianity he did find, had either lapsed into paganism or was mixed with error. The clergy were mainly responsible for these latter conditions since they were in many instances uneducated, lax and questionably obedient to their bishops. In particular instances, their very ordination was questionable.

These are the conditions that Boniface was to report in 722 on his first return visit to Rome. The Holy Father instructed him to reform the German Church. To fulfill these duties, he was made a Regional Bishop. The Pope sent letters of recommendation to religious and civil leaders. Boniface later admitted that his work would have been unsuccessful, from a human viewpoint, without a letter of safe conduct from Charles Martel. He was finally made a regional bishop and authorized to organize the whole German church. He was eminently successful.

In the Frankish kingdom, he met great problems because of lay interference in bishops' elections, the worldliness of the clergy, and lack of papal control.

During a final mission to the Frisians, he and 53 companions were massacred while he was preparing converts for Confirmation.

In order to restore the Germanic Church to its fidelity to Rome, and to convert the pagans, he had been guided by two principles. The first was to restore the obedience of the clergy to their bishops in union with the Pope of Rome. The second was the establishment of many houses of prayer which took the form of Benedictine monasteries. A great number of Anglo-Saxon monks and nuns followed him to the Continent. He introduced Benedictine nuns to the active apostolate of education.

COMMENT: Boniface bears out the Christian rule: to follow Christ is to follow the way of the cross. For Boniface, it was not only physical suffering or death, but the painful, thankless, bewildering task of church reform. Missionary glory is often thought of in terms of bringing new persons to Christ. It seems — but is not — less glorious to heal the household of the faith.

STORY: Boniface literally struck a blow for Christianity in his attempt to destroy pagan superstitions. On a day previously announced, in the presence of a tense crowd, he attacked with an axe Donar's sacred oak on Mount Gudenburg. The huge tree crashed, splitting into four parts. The people waited for the gods to strike Boniface dead — then realized their gods were powerless, non-existent. He used planks from the tree to build a chapel.

June 6   *Optional*

NORBERT, bishop
(1080? - 1134)

Friends sometimes jokingly mangle the name of the Premonstratensians into "Monstrous Pretensions," just as the Franciscan "O.F.M." is said to mean "Out For Money." The name actually derives from Premontre, the region of France where Norbert established the order in the 12th century.

Recalling the nick-name, Norbert's founding of the order was in truth a monstrous task: combatting rampant heresies particularly regarding the Blessed

Sacrament, revitalizing many of the faithful who had grown indifferent and dissolute and effecting peace and reconciliation among enemies.

Norbert entertained no pretensions about his own ability to accomplish this multiple task. Even with the aid of a goodly number of men who joined his order, he realized that nothing could be effectively done without God's power. Finding this help especially in devotion to the Blessed Sacrament, he and his Norbertines praised God for success in converting heretics, reconciling numerous enemies and rebuilding faith in indifferent believers.

Reluctantly, Norbert became Archbishop of Magdeburg in southern Germany, a territory half pagan and half Christian. In this position he zealously and courageously continued his work for the Church until his death on June 6, 1134.

COMMENT: A different world cannot be built by indifferent people. The same is true as regards the Church. Sad to say, the so-called updating of the Church has not engendered the different Church which was so devoutly and hopefully envisioned by Vatican Council II. A principal reason for this failure was — and is — the indifference of vast numbers of nominal faithful, their indifference for ecclesiastical authority, essential doctrines of the faith. Unswerving loyalty to the Church and fervent devotion to the Eucharist, as practiced by Norbert, will continue immeasurably towards maintaining the people of God in accord with the heart of Christ.

QUOTE: On the occasion of his ordination to the priesthood, Norbert said, "O Priest! You are not yourself because you are God. You are not of yourself because you are the servant and minister of Christ. You are not your own because you are the spouse of the Church. You are not yourself because you are the mediator between God and man. You are not from yourself because you are nothing. What then are you? Nothing and everything. O Priest! Take care lest what was said to Christ on the cross be said to you: 'He saved others, himself he cannot save!' "

EPHREM THE SYRIAN,
deacon and doctor
(306?-373)

Poet, teacher, orator and defender of the faith, Ephrem is the only Syrian ever to be acclaimed a Doctor of the Church. He took upon himself the special task of opposing the many false doctrines rampant at his time, always remaining a true and forceful defender of the Catholic Church.

Born in Nisibis, Mesopotamia, he was baptized as a young man and became famous as a teacher in his native city. When the Christian emperor had to cede Nisibis to the Persians, Ephrem, along with many Christians, fled as a refugee to Edessa. He is credited with attracting great glory to the biblical school there. He was ordained a deacon, but declined becoming a priest (and was said to have avoided episcopal consecration by feigning madness!).

He had a prolific pen and his writings best illumine his holiness. Although he was not a man of great scholarship, his works reflect deep insight and knowledge of the scriptures. In writing about the mysteries of man's redemption, Ephrem reveals a realistic and humanly sympathetic spirit and a great devotion to the humanity of Jesus and Mary. It is said that his poetic account of the Last Judgement inspired Dante.

It is surprising to read that he wrote hymns against the heretics of his day. He would take the popular songs of the heretical groups and, using their melodies, compose beautiful hymns embodying orthodox doctrine. Ephrem became one of the first to introduce song into the Church's public worship as a means of instruction for the faithful. His many hymns have earned him the title "Harp of the Holy Spirit."

He preferred a simple, austere life, living in a small cave overlooking the city of Edessa. It was here he died around 373.

COMMENT: Many Catholics still find singing in church a problem, probably because of the rather individualistic piety that they inherited. Yet singing has been a tradition of both the Old and the New Testament. It is an excellent way of expressing and creating a community spirit of unity, as well as joy. Ephrem's hymns, and ancient historian testifies, "lent luster to the Christian assemblies." We need some modern Ephrems — and cooperating singers — to do the same for our Christian assemblies today.

"Lay me not with sweet spices,
   For this honor avails me not,
Nor yet use incense and perfumes,
   For the honor befits me not.
Burn ye the incense in the holy place;
   As for me, escort me only with your prayers,
Give ye your incense to God,
   And over me send up hymns.
Instead of perfumes and spices,
   Be mindful of me in your intercessions."

June 11   *Memorial*

BARNABAS, apostle

Barnabas, a Jew of Cyprus, comes as close as anyone outside the Twelve to being a full-fledged Apostle. He was closely associated with St. Paul (he introduced Paul to Peter and the other apostles), and served as a kind of mediator between the former persecutor and the still suspicious Jewish Christians.

When a Christian community developed at Antioch, Barnabas was sent as the official representative of the mother church of Jerusalem to incorporate them into the fold. He and Paul instructed in Antioch for a year, after which they took relief contributions to Jerusalem.

Later, Paul and Barnabas, now clearly seen as charismatic leaders, were sent by Antioch officials to preach to the Gentiles. Enormous success crowned their efforts. After a miracle at Lystra, the people wanted to offer sacrifice to them as gods — Barnabas being Zeus, and Paul, Hermes — but the two said, "We are just men, bringing you the good news that will convert you to the living God."

But all was not peaceful. They were expelled from one town; they had to go to Jerusalem to clear up the ever-recurring controversy about circumcision; and even the best of friends can have differences. When Paul wanted to revisit the places they had evangelized, Barnabas wanted to take along John Mark, his cousin, author of the Gospel; but Paul insisted that since Mark had deserted them once, he was not fit to take along now. The disagreement that followed was so sharp that Barnabas and Paul separated, Barnabas taking Mark to Cyprus, Paul taking Silas to Syria. Later, they were reconciled — Paul, Barnabas and Mark.

When Paul withstood Peter for not eating with Gentiles for fear of his Jewish friends, we learn that "even Barnabas was swept away by their pretense."

COMMENT: Barnabas is spoken of simply as one who dedicated his life to the Lord. He was a man "filled with the Holy Spirit and faith. *Thereby* large numbers were added to the Lord." Even when he and Paul were expelled from Antioch in Pisidia, they were "filled with joy and the Holy Spirit."

STORY: Barnabas is mentioned by name as one of the generous members of the idyllic and extremely poor Church in Jerusalem: "The community of believers were of one heart and one mind. Everything was held in common. There was no one needy among them, for all who owned property or houses sold them and donated the proceeds. There was a certain Levite from Cyprus named Joseph, to whom the apostles gave the name Barnabas (meaning 'son of encouragement'). He sold a farm that he owned and made a donation of the money, laying it at the apostles' feet."

ANTHONY OF PADUA,
priest and doctor
(1195-1231)

The Gospel call to leave everything and follow Christ was the rule of Anthony's life. Over and over again God called him to something new in his plan. Each time Anthony responded with renewed zeal and self-sacrificing to serve his Lord Jesus more completely.

His journey as the servant of God began as a very young man when he decided to join the Augustinians, giving up a future of wealth and power to be a servant of God. Later, when the bodies of the first Franciscan martyrs went through the town where he was stationed, he was again filled with an intense longing to be one of those closest to Jesus himself: those who die for the Good News.

So Anthony entered the Franciscan Order and set out to preach to the Moors. But an illness prevented him from achieving this goal. He returned to Italy and was stationed in a small hermitage where he spent most of his time praying, reading the Scriptures and doing menial tasks.

The call of God came again at an ordination where no one was prepared to speak. The humble and obedient Anthony hesitantly accepted the task. The years of searching for Jesus in prayer, in reading Sacred Scripture and in serving him in poverty, chastity and obedience had prepared Anthony to allow the Spirit to use his talents. Anthony's sermon was astounding to those who expected an unprepared speech and knew not the power of the Spirit in giving men words.

Recognized as a great man of prayer and a great Scripture and theology scholar, Anthony became the first friar to teach theology to the other friars. Again he was called from that post to preach to the heretics, to use his profound knowledge of Scripture and theology to convert and reassure those who had been misled.

COMMENT: Anthony should be the patron of those who find their lives completely uprooted and sent in a new and unexpected direction. Like all saints, he is a perfect example of turning one's life completely over to Christ. God did with Anthony as he pleased — and what he pleased was a life of spiritual power and brilliance that still attracts admiration today. He whom popular devotion has nominated as finder of lost objects found himself by losing himself totally to the providence of God.

QUOTE: In his *Sermons*, Anthony says: "The saints are like the stars. In his Providence Christ conceals them in a hidden place that they may not shine before others when they might wish to do so. Yet they are always ready to exchange the quiet of contemplation for the works of mercy as soon as they perceive in their heart the invitation of Christ."

ROMUALD, abbot
(950?-1027)

After a wasted youth, Romuald saw his father kill a relative in a duel over property. In horror he fled to a monastery near Ravenna in Italy. After three years he was found to be uncomfortably holy by some of the monks, and was eased out.

He spent the next 30 years going about Italy founding monasteries and hermitages. Like many others, he longed to give his life to Christ in martyrdom, and got the Pope's permission to preach the Gospel in Hungary. But he was struck with illness as soon as he arrived, and the illness recurred as often as he tried to proceed.

During another period of his life, he suffered great spiritual dryness. One day as he was praying Psalm 31 ("I will give you understanding and I will instruct you"), he was given an extraordinary light and spirit which never left him.

At the next monastery where he stayed, he was accused of a scandalous crime by a young nobleman he had rebuked for a dissolute life. Amazingly, his fellow monks believe the accusation. He was given a severe penance, forbidden to offer Mass and excommunicated. After six months of silence, he knew that he should no longer submit to so unjust a sentence.

The most famous of the monasteries he founded

was that of the Camaldoli (Campus Maldoli, name of the owner) in Tuscany. Here he founded the order of the Camaldolese Benedictines, uniting a monastic and hermit life.

His father later became a monk, wavered, and was kept faithful by the encouragement of his son.

COMMENT: Christ is a gentle leader, but he calls us to total holiness. Now and then men and women are rised up to challenge us by the absoluteness of their dedication, the vigor of their spirit, the depth of their conversion. The fact that we cannot duplicate their lives does not change the call to us to be totally open to God in our own particular circumstances.

STORY: A Polish duke had a son in the monastery where Romuald was living. The son, on behalf of his father, presented Romuald with a fine horse. Romuald exchanged it for a donkey, saying that he felt closer to Jesus Christ on such a mount.

June 21   *Memorial*
ALOYSIUS GONZAGA, religious
(1568-1591)

The Lord can make saints anywhere, even amid the brutality and license of Renaissance life. Florence was the "mother of piety" for Aloysius Gonzaga despite his exposure to a "society of fraud, dagger, poison and lust." As a son of a princely family, he grew up in royal courts and army camps. His father wanted Aloysius to be a military hero.

139

At 7 he experienced a profound spiritual quickening. His prayers included the Office of Mary, the psalms and other devotions. At 9 he came from his hometown of Castiglione to Florence to be educated; by 11 he was teaching catechism to poor children, fasting three days a week and practicing great austerities. When he was 13 he traveled with his parents and the Empress of Austria to Spain and acted as a page in the court of Philip II. The more Aloysius saw of court life, the more he was turned off, seeking relief in learning about the lives of saints.

A book about the experiences of Jesuit missionaries in India suggested to him the idea of entering the Society of Jesus, and in Spain his decision became final. Now began a four-year contest with his father. Eminent churchmen and laymen were pressed into service to persuade him to remain in his "normal" vocation. Finally he prevailed, was allowed to renounce his right of succession and was received into the Jesuit novitiate.

Like other seminarians, he was faced with a new kind of penance — that of accepting different ideas about the exact nature of penance.

He was obliged to eat more, take recreation with the other students. He was forbidden to pray except at stated times. He spent four years in the study of philosophy and had St. Robert Bellarmine as his spiritual adviser.

In 1591, a plague struck Rome. The Jesuits opened a hospital of their own, the general himself and many other Jesuits rendered personal service. Because he nursed patients, washing them and making their beds, Aloysius caught the disease himself. A fever persisted after recovery and he was so weak he could scarcely rise from bed. Yet, he maintained his great discipline of prayer, knowing that he would die within the octave of Corpus Christi. Three months later he died at 23.

COMMENT: As a saint who fasted, scourged himself, sought solitude and prayer, and did not look on the faces of women, Aloysius seems an unlikely patron of youth in a society where asceticism is confined to training camps of football teams and boxers, and sexual permissiveness has little left to permit. Can an overweight and air-conditioned society deprive itself of *anything*? It will when it discovers a reason, as Aloysius did. The motivation for letting God purify us is the experience of God loving us, in prayer.

QUOTE: "When we stand praying, beloved brethern, we ought to be watchful and earnest with our whole heart, intent on our prayers. Let all carnal and worldly thoughts pass away, nor let the soul at that time think on anything except the object of its prayer." (St. Cyprian, *On the Lord's Prayer*, 31).

June 22   *Optional*

PAULINUS OF NOLA, bishop
(354?-431)

Anyone who is praised in the letters of six or seven saints undoubtedly must be of extraordinary character. Such a person was Paulinus of Nola, correspondent and friend of Augustine, Jerome, Melania, Martin, Gregory and Ambrose.

Born near Bordeaux, he was the son of the Roman prefect of Gaul who had extensive property in both Gaul and Italy. Paulinus became a distinguished lawyer, holding several public offices in the Empire. With his Spanish wife Therasia, he retired at an early age to a life of cultured leisure.

The two were baptized by the saintly bishop of Bordeaux and moved to Therasia's estate in Spain. After many childless years, they had a son who died a week after birth. This occasioned their beginning a life of great austerity and charity, giving away most of their Spanish property. Possibly as a result of this great example, Paulinus was rather unexpectedly ordained priest at Christmas by the bishop of Barcelona.

He and his wife then moved to Nola, near Naples. He had a great love for St. Felix of Nola, and spent much effort in promoting devotion to the saint. He gave away most of his remaining property (to the consternation of his relatives) and continued his work for the poor. Supporting a host of debtors, tramps and other needy people, he lived a monastic life in another part of his home. By popular demand he was made bishop of Nola and guided that diocese for 21 years.

His last years were saddened by the invasion of the Huns. Among his few writings is the earliest extant Christian wedding song.

COMMENT: Many of us are tempted to "retire" early in life, after an initial burst of energy. Devotion to Christ and to his work is waiting to be done all around us. Paulinus' life had scarcely begun when he thought it was over, as he took his ease on that estate in Spain. Man proposes, but God disposes.

STORY: An eyewitness described Paulinus' last days: A priest came to him three days before his death, saying that 40 pieces of silver were needed for the poor. He smiled and said that someone would pay the debt of the poor. Almost immediately a messenger came with a gift of 50 silver pieces. On his last day, when the lamps were being lighted for Vespers, after having said nothing for a long time, he stretched out his hands and said, "I have prepared a lamp for my Christ."

June 22 *Optional*

JOHN FISHER, bishop and martyr
(1469-1535)

John Fisher is usually associated with Erasmus, Thomas More and other Renaissance humanists. His life, therefore, did not have the external simplicity found in the lives of some saints. Rather, he was a man of learning, associated with the intellectuals and political men of his day. He was interested in the contemporary culture and eventually became Chancellor at Cambridge. He had been made a bishop at 35, and one of his specific interests was in raising the standard of preaching in England. Fisher himself was an accomplished preacher and writer. His sermons on the penitential psalms were reprinted seven times before his death. With the coming of

Lutheranism, he was drawn into controversy. His eight books against heresy gave him a leading position among European theologians.

In 1527 he was asked to study the problem of Henry VIII's marriage. He incurred Henry's anger by defending the validity of his marriage with Catherine, and, later, by rejecting Henry's claim to being the supreme head of the Church in England.

In an attempt to be rid of him, Henry first had him accused of not reporting all the "revelations" of the nun of Kent, Elizabeth Barton. He was summoned, in feeble health, to take the oath to the new Act of Succession. He and Thomas More refused because the other presumed the legality of Henry's divorce and his claim to be head of the English church. They were sent to the Tower, where Fisher remained 14 months without trial. They were finally sentenced to life imprisonment and loss of goods.

When the two were called to further interrogations, they remained silent. Fisher was tricked, on the supposition he was speaking privately as a priest, and declared again that the king was not supreme head. The king, further angered that the Pope had made John Fisher a cardinal, had him brought to trial on the charge of high treason. He was condemned and executed, his body left to lie all day on the scaffold, and his head hung on London Bridge. More was executed two weeks later.

COMMENT: Today many questions are raised about Christians' and priests' active involvement in social issues. John Fisher remained faithful to his calling as a bishop. He strongly upheld the teachings of the Church — the very cause of his martyrdom was his loyalty to Rome. He was involved in the cultural enrichment circles as well as in the political struggles of his time. This involvement caused him to question the moral conduct of the leadership of his country. "The Church has the right, indeed the duty, to proclaim justice on the social, national and international level, and to denounce instances of injustice, when the fundamental rights of man and his very salvation demand it" (Justice in the World, Synod of Bishops, 1971).

QUOTE: Erasmus said of John Fisher: "He is the one man at this time who is incomparable for uprightness of life, for learning and for greatness of soul."

June 22   *Optional*

THOMAS MORE, martyr
(1478-1535)

His belief that no lay ruler has jurisdiction over the Church of Christ cost Thomas More his life.

Beheaded on Tower Hill, London, June 6, 1535, he steadfastly refused to approve Henry VIII's divorce and remarriage and establishment of the Church of England.

Described as "a man for all seasons," More was a literary scholar, emminent lawyer, gentleman, father of four children, and chancellor of England. An intensely spiritual man, he would not support the king's divorce from Catherine of Aragon in order to marry Anne Boleyn. Nor would he acknowledge Henry as supreme head of the Church in England, breaking with Rome and denying the pope as head.

He was committed to the Tower of London to await trial for treason: not swearing to the Act of Succession and the Oath of Supremacy. Upon conviction, More declared he had all the councils of Christendom and not just the council of one realm to support him in the decision of his conscience.

COMMENT: Four hundred years later, in 1935, Thomas More was canonized a saint of God. Few saints are more relevant to the 20th century. The supreme diplomat and counsellor, he did not compromise his own moral values in order to please the king, knowing that true allegiance to authority is not blind acceptance of everything the authority wants. Henry himself realized this and tried desperately to win his chancellor to his side because he knew More was a man whose approval counted, a man whose personal integrity no one questioned. But when Thomas resigned as chancellor, unable to approve the two matters that meant most to Henry, Henry had to get rid of Thomas.

STORY: When the executioner offered to blindfold him, More said that he would do this himself. But after he had stretched his head over the low block — it was merely a log of wood — he made a signal to the man to wait a moment. Then he made his last joke: his beard was lying on the block; he would like to remove it. At least *that* had committed no treason. The heavy axe went slowly up, hung a moment in the air and fell (Theodore Maynard, *Humanist as Hero*).

BIRTH OF JOHN THE BAPTIST

Jesus called John the greatest of all those who had preceded him: "History has not known a man born of woman greater than John the Baptizer." But John would have agreed completely with what Jesus added: "Yet the least born into the kingdom of God is greater than he."

John spent his time in the desert, an ascetic. He began to announce the coming of the Kingdom, and to call everyone to a fundamental reformation of life.

His purpose was to prepare the way for Jesus. His baptism, he said, was for repentance. But One would come who would baptize with the Holy Spirit and fire. John is not worthy even to carry his sandals. His attitude toward Jesus was: "He must increase, I must decrease" (John 3,30).

He was humbled to find, among the crowd of sinners who came to be baptized, the one whom he already knew to be the Messiah. "You are the one who should baptize me!" But Jesus insisted, "Give in for now. We must do this if we are to fulfill all of God's commands." Jesus, true and humble man as well as eternal God, was eager to do what was required of any good Jew. John was proclaiming the coming of the Kingdom. Jesus now publicly enters the community of those awaiting the Messiah. By making himself part of that community, he makes it truly messianic.

The greatness of John, his pivotal place in the history of salvation, is seen in the great emphasis Luke gives to the annunication of his birth and the event itself — both made prominently parallel to the same occurrences in the life of Jesus. He attracted countless people ("all Judea") to the banks of the Jordan, and it occurred to some people that he might be the Messiah. But he constantly deferred to Jesus, even to sending away some of his followers to become the first disciples of Jesus.

Perhaps John's idea of the coming of the Kingdom was not being perfectly fulfilled in the public ministry of Jesus. For whatever reason, he sent his disciples (when he was in prison) to ask Jesus if he was the Messiah. Jesus' answer showed that the Messiah was to be a figure like that of the Suffering Servant in Isaiah. John himself would share in the pattern of messianic suffering, losing his life to the revenge of Herodias.

COMMENT: John challenges us Christians to the fundamental attitude of Christianity — total dependence of the Father, in Christ. Except for the Mother of God, no one had a higher function in the unfolding of salvation. Yet the least in the kingdom, Jesus said, is greater than he, for the pure gift that the Father gives. The attractiveness as well as the austerity of John, his fierce courage in denouncing evil, all stem from his fundamental and total placing of his life within the will of God.

QUOTE: "And this is not something which was only true once, long ago in the past. It is always true, because the repentance which he preached always remains the way into the kingdom which he announced. He is not a figure that we can forget now that Jesus, the true light, has appeared. John is always relevant because he calls for a preparation which all men need to make. Hence every year there are four weeks in the life of the Church in which it listens to the voice of the Baptist. These are the weeks of Advent" (*A New Catechism*).

CYRIL OF ALEXANDRIA,
bishop and doctor
(376?-444)

Saints are not born with haloes around their heads. Cyril, recognized as a great teacher of the Church, began his career as archbishop of Alexandria (Egypt) with impulsive, often violent, actions. He pillaged and closed the churches of the Novatian heretics, participated in the deposing of St. John Chrysostom and confiscated Jewish property, expelling the Jews from Alexandria in retaliation for their attacks on Christians.

Cyril's importance for theology and Church history lies in his championing the cause of orthodoxy against the heresy of Nestorius.

The controversy centered around the two natures in Christ. Nestorius would not agree to the word "God-bearer" for Mary. He preferred "Christ-bearer," saying there are two distinct persons in Christ (divine and human) joined only by a moral union. He said Mary was not the mother of God but only of the man Christ, whose humanity was only a temple of God. Nestorianism implied that the humanity of Christ was a mere disguise.

Cyril, presiding as the Pope's representative at the Council of Ephesus (431), condemned Nestorianism and proclaimed Mary truly the "God-bearer" (the mother of the one Person who is truly God and truly man). In the confusion that followed, Cyril was deposed and imprisoned for three months, after which he was welcomed back to Alexandria as a second Athanasius (the champion against Arianism).

Besides needing to soften some of his opposition to those who had sided with Nestorius, Cyril had difficulties with some of his own allies, who thought he had gone too far, sacrificing not only language but orthodoxy. Until his death, his policy of moderation kept his extreme partisans under control. On his deathbed, despite pressure, he refused to condemn the teacher of Nestorius.

COMMENT: Lives of the saints are valuable not only for the virtue they reveal but also for the less admirable qualities that also appear. Holiness is a gift of God to us as human beings. Life is a process. We respond to God's gift, but sometimes with a lot of zigzagging. If Cyril had been more patient and diplomatic, the Nestorian Church might not have risen and maintained power so long. But even saints must grow out of immaturity, narrowness and selfishness. It is because they — and we — do grow, that we are truly saints, persons who live the life of God.

QUOTE: Cyril's theme: "Only if it is one and the same Christ who is consubstantial with the Father and with men can he save us, for the meeting ground between God and man is the flesh of Christ. Only if this is God's own flesh can man come into contact with Christ's divinity through his humanity. Because of our kinship with the Word made flesh we are sons of God. The Eucharist consummates our kinship with the Word, our communion with the Father, our sharing in the divine nature — there is a very real

contact between our body and that of the Word"
(*New Catholic Encyclopedia*).

IRENAEUS, bishop and martyr
(130?-220)

The Church is fortunate that Irenaeus was involved in much of its controversy in the second century. He was a student, well trained, no doubt, with
great patience in investigating, tremendously protec-
tive of apostolic teaching, but prompted more by a
desire to win over his opponents than to prove them
in error.

As bishop of Lyons he was especially concerned
with the Gnostics, whose teaching was attracting and
confusing many of the Gallic Christians. After
thoroughly investigating the various Gnostic sects
and their "secrets", he set about showing to what
logical conclusions their tenets led. These he con-
trasted with the teaching of the Apostles and the text
of Holy Scripture, giving us, in five books, a system
of theology of great importance to subsequent times.
Moreover, his work, widely used and translated into
Latin and Armenian, gradually ended the influence
of the Gnostics.

The circumstances and manner of his death, like
those of his birth and early life in Asia Minor, are
not at all clear.

COMMENT: A deep and genuine concern for
fellow men will remind us that the discovery of truth

is not to be a victory for some and a defeat for others. Unless all can claim a share in that victory, truth itself will continue to be rejected by the losers, because it will be regarded as inseparable from the yoke of defeat. And so, confrontation, controversy, etc., must yield to a genuine united search for God's truth and how it can best be served.

STORY: A group of Christians in Asia Minor had been put under the ban of excommunication by Pope Victor III because of their refusal to accept the date of the Western Church for the celebration of Easter. Irenaeus, the "lover of peace" as his name indicates, interceded with the pope to lift the ban, indicating that this was not an essential matter and that these people were merely following an old tradition, one that men such as St. Polycarp and Pope Anicetus had not seen as divisive. The pope responded favorably and the rift was healed. Some one hundred years later, the Western practice was voluntarily adopted.

June 29   *Solemnity*

PETER and PAUL, apostles

Peter (d. 64?)

St. Mark ends the first half of his gospel with a triumphant climax. He has recorded doubt, misunderstanding and the opposition of many to Jesus. Now Peter makes his great confession of faith: "You are the Messiah!"

It was one of the many glorious moments in

Peter's life, beginning with the day he was called from his nets along the Sea of Galilee to become a fisher of men for Jesus.

The New Testament clearly shows Peter as the leader of the apostles, chosen by Jesus to have a special relationship with him. With James and John he was privileged to witness the Transfiguration, the raising of a dead child to life and the agony in Gethsemani. His mother-in-law was cured by Jesus. He was sent with John to prepare for the last Passover before Jesus' death. His name is first on every list of apostles.

And to him only was it said, "Blessed are you, Simon . . . No mere man has revealed this to you, but my heavenly Father. I for my part declare to you, you are Rock, and on this Rock I will build my church, and the jaws of death shall not prevail against it. I will entrust to you the keys of the kingdom of heaven. Whatever you declare bound on earth shall be bound in heaven. Whatever you declare loosed on earth shall be loosed in heaven."

But the Gospels prove their own veracity by the unflattering details they include about Peter. He clearly had no PR man. It is a great comfort for ordinary mortals to know that Peter also had his human weakness, even in the presence of Jesus.

He had generously given up all things, yet he could ask, in childish self-regard, "What are we going to get for all this?" He receives the full force of Christ's anger when he objects to the idea of a suffering Messiah: "Get out of my sight, you satan, you enemy! You are trying to make me trip and fall! You are not judging by God's standards, "but by man's."

Peter is willing to accept Jesus' doctrine of forgiveness, but suggests a limit of seven times. He walks on the water in faith, but sinks in doubt. He refuses to let Jesus wash his feet, then wants his whole body cleansed. He swore at the Last Supper that he would never deny Jesus, and then swore to a servant maid that he had never known the man. He loyally resisted the first attempt to arrest Jesus by cutting off Malchus' ear, but in the end he ran away with the others. In the depth of his sorrow, Jesus looked on him and forgave him, and he went out and shed bitter tears.

COMMENT: We would probably go to confession to Peter sooner than to any of the other apostles. He is perhaps a more striking example of the simple fact of holiness: "It is not you who have chosen me, but I who have chosen you. Peter, it is not human wisdom that makes it possible for you to believe, but my Father's revelation. I, not you, build my church."

QUOTE: "Bow humbly under God's mighty hand, so that in due time he may lift you high. Cast all your cares on him because he cares for you. Stay sober and alert. Your opponent the devil is prowling like a roaring lion looking for someone to devour. Resist him, solid in your faith, realizing that the brotherhood of believers is undergoing the same sufferings throughout the world. The God of all grace, who has called you to his everlasting glory in Christ, will himself restore, confirm, strengthen and establish those who have suffered a little while" (First Letter of Peter, 5:6-10).

Paul (d. 64?)

If Billy Graham suddenly began preaching that the U.S. should adopt Marxism and not rely on the Constitution, the angry reaction would help us understand Paul's life when he started preaching that Christ alone can save us. He had been the most Pharisaic of Pharisees, the most legalistic of Mosaic lawyers. Now he suddenly appears to his brother Jews as a heretical welcomer of Gentiles, a traitor and apostate.

Paul's central conviction was simple and absolute: Only God can save man. No human effort — even the most scrupulous observance of Law can create a human good which we can bring to God as reparation for sin and payment for grace. To be saved from himself, from sin, from the devil and from death, man must open himself completely to the saving power of Jesus.

Paul never lost his love for his brother Jews, though he carried on a lifelong debate with them about the uselessness of the Law without Christ. He reminded the Gentiles that they were grafted on the parent stock of the Jews, who were still God's chosen people, the children of the promise.

His experiencing the personal risen Jesus on the road to Damascus was the driving force that made him one of the most zealous, dynamic and courageous ambassadors of Christ the Church has ever had. But persecution, humiliation and weakness became his day-by-day carrying of the Cross, material for further transformation. The dying Christ was in him; the living Christ was his life.

It is ironic, perhaps, that after a lifetime of suffering for Christ at the hands of his fellow Jews, and working for Gentile conversion, he should be martyred at the hands of Gentile power, the Roman Emperor Nero.

COMMENT: Paul did his best, without compromise, to unify a polarized Jewish-Gentile Church. One of his greatest gestures was a collection taken up among the Gentile churches to aid the poor mother church in Jerusalem, Jewish Christians. It was first a means of relieving their material need; it was also a symbolic statement of the solidarity among all Christians. Paul probably never overcame entirely the suspicion of Jewish Christians. Yet, whatever his Christlike failures, he was the instrument Christ used to save Christianity from slavery to the Law as a means of salvation, and to enrich the newly engrafted Gentile branches with the precious heritage of the Jews.

QUOTE: Paul's talks about his sufferings: "Five times at the hands of the Jews I received 40 lashes less one; three times I was beaten with rods; I was stoned once, shipwrecked three times; I passed a day and a night on the sea. I traveled continually, endangered by floods, robbers, my own people, the Gentiles; imperiled in the city, in the desert, at the sea, by false brothers; enduring labor, hardship, many sleepless nights; in hunger and thirst, in frequent fastings, in cold and nakedness . . . I am content with weakness, with mistreatment, with distress, with persecutions and difficulties for the sake of Christ; for when I am powerless, then it is then that I am strong" (II Cor. 11:24-27; 12:10).

INDEX OF SAINTS, vol. I